# INTRODUCING THE CATECHISM OF THE CATHOLIC CHURCH

## Traditional Themes and Contemporary Issues

*edited by*
Berard L. Marthaler

PAULIST PRESS
New York, NY • Mahwah, NJ

Library of Congress Cataloging-in-Publication Data

Introducing the Catechism of the Catholic Church / edited by Berard L. Marthaler.
    p.   cm.
  Includes bibliographical references.
  ISBN 0-8091-3495-0
  1. Catholic Church. Catechismus Ecclesiae Catholicae.   2. Catholic
Church—Catechisms.  I. Marthaler, Berard L.
BX 1959.5.I58   1994
238'.2—dc20                                94-2648
                                            CIP

Published by Paulist Press
997 Macarthur Boulevard
Mahwah, New Jersey 07430

Printed and bound in the
United States of America

# CONTENTS

**Mary Collins and Berard L. Marthaler**
Preface............................................................v

**John E. Pollard**
Introduction.......................................................1

**Berard L. Marthaler**
The Ecclesial Context of the Catechism..........................5

**Joseph A. Komonchak**
The Authority of the Catechism.................................18

**Gerard S. Sloyan**
The Role of the Bible in Catechesis
According to the Catechism.....................................32

**Berard L. Marthaler**
Does the Catechism Reflect a Hierarchy of Truths? ............43

**Peter C. Phan**
What Is Old and What Is New in the Catechism? ...............56

**John Borelli**
The Catechism and Interreligious Dialogue:
The Jews and World Religions .................................72

**Catherine Dooley**
Liturgical Catechesis According to the Catechism..............87

**Robert M. Friday**
The Formation of Conscience
According to the Catechism.....................................99

**James L. Nash**
Catechesis for Justice and Peace in the Catechism ............112

**Gerard S. Sloyan**
The Homily and Catechesis:
The Catechism and/or the Lectionary? ......................133

**Virgil Elizondo**
Cultural Pluralism and the Catechism ........................142

**Notes**.......................................................163

**Contributors** .................................................181

# PREFACE

The publication this spring of an authorized English translation makes the *Catechism of the Catholic Church* accessible, at long last, to the Anglophone world. The document witnesses to the Catholic faith that comes to us from the apostles. It attempts to capture within the covers of a book, albeit a volume of almost 600 pages, the spirit and substance of the Christian message revealed in and by Christ, and to witness to nineteen centuries of tradition and practice within the Christian community.

The Synod of Bishops, convened in 1985 to mark the twentieth anniversary of the conclusion of Vatican II, endorsed a proposal made by Cardinal Bernard Law of Boston calling for "a catechism or compendium of all Catholic doctrine regarding both faith and morals." The Synod recommended that "the presentation of doctrine should be biblical and liturgical, presenting sure teaching adapted to the actual life of Christians." Pope John Paul entrusted the task of preparing a plan for the Catechism to a commission of twelve cardinals and bishops, assisted by an editorial committee of seven diocesan bishops, experts in theology and experienced in catechesis, who were to carry out the work. After compiling several drafts and after worldwide consultation, they completed their work in the summer of 1992.

Pope John Paul II prefaced the *Catechism of the Catholic Church* with the apostolic constitution *Fidei Depositum* (October 11, 1992). In promulgating the text he stated that, like the master of the household in Matthew's gospel, the Catechism brings out the old and the new. The old is embedded in the structure of the "four pillars" canonized by the *Roman Catechism* of Pius V (1566): the Creed, the Sacraments, the Commandments, and the Lord's Prayer. The new is represented by the way the Catechism engages "questions of our time." It is like a modern museum that displays cultural artifacts and *objets d'art* from every epoch, from ancient to contemporary. The Catechism is replete with pictures from the catacombs, patristic texts, axioms from medieval scholasticism, references to the Council of Trent, and quotations from sources such as the autobiography of St. Teresa of Avila and the writings of Cardinal Newman. Next to the Holy Scriptures, the documents of the Second Vatican Council are the texts most often cited.

The original French text of the Catechism was followed almost immediately by an Italian translation and shortly thereafter by Spanish and German translations. Many factors, including honest differences over the principles that should guide the translation, and an organized effort led by a group of dissidents who had their own agenda, delayed the appearance of an authorized English text. With every reason to believe that an English translation would be available in the spring of 1993, the School of Religious Studies at The Catholic University of America planned a symposium to showcase the Catechism and to provide background that would help publishers, diocesan personnel, and parish directors of religious education in appreciating its breadth, depth, and, on some points, its self-imposed limitations. The speakers for the most part were faculty members of the Department of Religion and Religious Education, but they also included the Reverend Peter Phan, chair of the Department of Theology, Dr. John Borelli of the USCC Department of Ecumenical and Interreligious Affairs, and the Reverend Virgilio Elizondo of the Mexican American Cultural Center. The remarks of Father John Pollard, representative for catechesis and leadership in the USCC Department of Education, introduce this collection and capture the intent and spirit of the symposium.

The symposium was not designed to provide either a systematic commentary or a critique of the Catechism. The speakers were asked to address issues that had been raised in connection with the Catechism: How do we reconcile the proposal of the Synod with Vatican II's refusal to authorize a catechism for the universal Church? What is its teaching authority? How does it use Scripture? What is "old" and what is "new" in its treatment of doctrine, liturgy, and Christian life? What does it say about ecumenism, Jewish–Christian relations, and dialogue with world religions? Does it make allowance for cultural diversity and differences in developmental stages? Some papers provide a context for the interpretation of the Catechism, some single out themes that seem to provide the warp and woof of its teaching. A few authors criticize the text for the way it presents specific points of doctrine, some fault it for what it does not say, but overall the authors were positive in their assessment. They agreed that the Catechism can indeed become, in the words of Pope John Paul II, "a valuable and authorized instrument at the service of the ecclesial communion and a sure and certain standard for the teaching of the faith."

Despite (or perhaps because of) the fact that an authorized English text of the Catechism was not available, the symposium was over-subscribed. At the close of the symposium participants urged that the papers be published. We delayed in putting the papers into print on the assumption that an authorized English text would be available by the end of 1993. When it became evident that such would not be the case, we decided to proceed with publication so that the papers would be available when the English translation does appear. Thus the quotations from the Catechism are not uniform. Some authors made their own translations from the French, Spanish, and Italian editions, but most used an unauthorized translation that was in circulation.

In this context it should be noted that one paper that was part of the symposium does not appear. Father Douglas Clark from Savannah, Georgia, who headed the team that was originally charged with producing an English version of the Catechism, explained the challenges of translating the text and the principles that guided the work.[1] Subsequently those principles were challenged and modified. Further reflection and the final word on "Englishing the Catechism" must be left to a later time.

Although the success of a symposium of this kind is measured by the quality of the papers and the interest of the participants, it depends also on the contributions of many whose names do not appear in the table of contents. Helen Didion, the efficient secretary of the Department of Religion and Religious Education, managed the administrative details. Graduate students headed by Charles Parr and Sabrina Karsanac took care of practical needs. Morris

---

[1] See the essay by Douglas K. Clark, "On 'Englishing' the Catechism," in *The Living Light* 29 (Summer 1993): 13–28.

Pelzel, master of the word-processor and dependable copy-editor, prepared the manuscripts for publication. To these and all who contributed to the success of the symposium we express our thanks.

MARY COLLINS, O.S.B.
*Chair, Department of Religion and Religious Education*

BERARD L. MARTHALER, OFMConv.
*Warren-Blanding Professor of Religion*

# INTRODUCTION

## John E. Pollard

I have been asked to make some brief introductory remarks regarding the essays in this volume on the *Catechism of the Catholic Church*. I shall make three brief comments on the intended audience of the Catechism, the purpose of the Catechism, and the "indispensable necessity of mediation" of the Catechism.

The Catechism is intended primarily for bishops, as teachers of the faith and pastors of the church. They have the first responsibility in catechesis. Through the bishops it is addressed to authors, publishers, and editors of national and local catechisms, to priests, catechists, and all others responsible for catechesis. It will also be useful reading for the faithful.

The bishops of the United States have established a Committee to Plan the Implementation of the Catechism. It is the committee's responsibility to suggest ways that the Catechism might be integrated into the catechetical mission of the National Conference of Catholic Bishops itself and into the catechetical missions of the individual dioceses in this country. It is not the responsibility of this committee to develop a plan that must be followed by individual dioceses. Among the suggestions that have been made is the sponsorship of symposia, workshops, and study days by dioceses, universities, and national educational and catechetical organizations. The essays in this collection were originally presented at a workshop sponsored by the Department of Religion and Religious Education, The Catholic University of America.

On the international level, the Congregation for the Clergy, with whom the responsibility for the oversight of catechetics rests, also recently held a meeting of all the presidents of the catechetical commissions of national episcopal conferences throughout the world to initiate the worldwide implementation of the Catechism. The U.S. episcopal conference was represented by Bishop John Leibrecht, chairman of the Bishops' Committee on Education, who presented a full report on the implementation plans of the U.S. bishops.

The Catechism serves several important functions:

1) It conveys the essential and fundamental content of Catholic faith and morals in a complete and summary way.
2) It is a point of reference for national and diocesan catechisms.
3) It is a positive, objective, and declarative exposition of Catholic doctrine.
4) It is intended to assist those who have the duty to catechize, namely, promoters and teachers of catechesis.

The *Catechism of the Catholic Church* presents what Catholics in all parts of the world believe in common. The national or diocesan catechisms and other catechetical material that may be developed in light of the *Catechism of the Catholic Church* will naturally be more sensitive to local cultural, social, and ecclesial concerns. The Catechism aims to foster the unity of faith, not the uniformity of expression of faith. The Holy Father has called the Catechism "a gift for the church," not a straitjacket for the church.

Lastly, the "indispensable necessity of mediation." The *Catechism of the Catholic Church* is addressed to the whole church as it is experienced in different places throughout the world. Therefore it cannot embody all the distinctive and specific aspects of the multiform local churches. It cannot express the unique characteristics of the different cultures around the world or the particular characteristics proper to every person's developmental level. Hence, it requires the "indispensable necessity of mediation" of national and diocesan catechisms and other catechetical materials.

Authors, editors, and publishers of national or diocesan catechisms and other catechetical materials should pay particular attention to the different social, cultural, and ecclesial contexts and to the unique characteristics of the persons to whom the catechesis is directed as they seek to mediate the content of the Catechism.

The Catechism is not intended for direct use by young adults, youth, and children. Neither does it include pedagogical or methodological considerations. Methodology varies according to the developmental levels of those to whom the catechesis is directed and according to the cultural contexts in which catechesis is given. Methodology is more appropriately developed by the authors and publishers of catechetical materials.

These essays can be a helpful aid in integrating the content of the Catechism into the catechetical mission of the church in the United States. This is just the kind of examination and inquiry that carefully and responsibly probes the Catechism and discovers those themes that have particular significance for the multicultural and pluralistic Catholic Church of the United States.

# THE ECCLESIAL CONTEXT
# OF THE CATECHISM

# Berard L. Marthaler

The most significant action taken by the Extraordinary Assembly of the Synod of Bishops that convened in 1985 to commemorate the twentieth anniversary of the Second Vatican Council was the recommendation that led in time to the publication of the *Catechism of the Catholic Church*. The wording of that resolution, as we shall see below, is significant. It asked that "a catechism or compendium of all Catholic doctrine regarding both faith and morals be composed, that it might be, as it were, a point of reference for the catechisms or compendiums that are prepared in the various countries." The resolution was a result of the proposal made by Cardinal Bernard Law of Boston on the floor of the synod for a "conciliar catechism." Suggestions of this kind had been put forward many times in the years before and after Vatican II, but they were never acted upon. What had changed in the ecclesial world to gain acceptance for a proposal similar to ones that had been ignored, not to say rejected, by previous synods?

In order to appreciate the significance of this shift in attitude and policy, it necessary to review the position taken by the Second Council of the Vatican regarding a catechism for the universal church.

## VATICAN II: PROPOSALS FOR A CATECHISM[1]

In 1961–62, when preparations for the council were underway and schemas were being drafted, the Central Preparatory Commission—the steering committee—instructed the Preparatory Commission *de disciplina cleri et populi Christiani* 1) to draw up plans for a new catechism containing the principal elements of the sacred liturgy, church history, and the social teachings of the church;

and 2) to give a new impetus to catechesis for adults. The commission *de disciplina* responded by drafting a schema that endorsed the notion of a general directory—guidelines—rather than a catechism for the universal church. It had three chapters: I. *De catechismo et de libris catechistis* ("The Catechism and Catechetical Books"); II. *De institutionis catecheticae organizatione* ("The Organization of Catechetical Instruction"); and III. *De methodo institutionis catecheticae trahendae* ("The Method To Be Used in Catechetical Instruction").

Meanwhile two other preparatory commissions were formulating proposals that dealt with catechesis. The Preparatory Commission for the Eastern Churches drafted the schema "The Catechism and Catechetical Instruction." It argued that the diversity in the world today makes it ever more necessary to insure uniform teaching and learning about Christian doctrine. The commission urged a kind of "compendium" that would serve as a catechism for the universal church, giving due respect to the Oriental rites.

The Preparatory Commission for the Sacraments drafted an eight-page schema, "Preparation for Marriage." It took the position that since the church insists on catechetical instruction for adults receiving baptism and confirmation, there should be *a pari* prenuptial catechesis that includes an examination on doctrine.

The Central Preparatory Commission folded the three proposals into a new schema *De cura animarum* ("The Care of Souls") that after several permutations emerged as the council's Decree on the Pastoral Office of Bishops, *Christus Dominus,* approved in the last year of the council. Article 44 of the decree, something of a catch-all, presented a general mandate prescribing the revision of the Code of Canon Law, general directories for different forms of pastoral care, and a general directory treating "the catechetical education of the Christian people, and should deal with fundamental principles of such education, its organization and the composition of books on the subject." Article 44 adds, "In preparation of these directories, special attention is to be given to the views which have been expressed by individual commissions and fathers of the council."

The various commissions and fathers of the council, though they expressed concern about teaching common doctrine and the need to memorize basic prayers, showed little enthusiasm for a catechism for the universal church. They discouraged diocesan cat-echisms in favor of national and regional catechisms authorized by episcopal conferences. A General Catechetical Directory, it was thought, would insure the integrity of catechesis by establishing basic principles, norms concerning the content of catechesis, guide-lines for authors and programs, and assistance in the drafting of national and regional catechisms. Pope Paul VI gave the task of implementing this decree to the Congregation of the Clergy.

## THE SYNOD OF BISHOPS CONSIDERS A CATECHISM[2]

The first assembly of the Synod of Bishops met in the fall of 1967 when the uproar over the Dutch Catechism was at its peak. In his inaugural address Pope Paul VI summoned the bishops to insure the integrity of the Catholic faith, renew its vigor, and ad-dress the dangers that threatened it. Several bishops, as a way of achieving these aims, proposed a catechism like that of the Coun-cil of Trent; one or the other bishop proposed a revised edition of the Tridentine Catechism that would incorporate the teachings of Vatican II; others favored a catechism for adults, but they were vague as to its nature and contents. In the end, however, no action was taken on a catechism because, most agreed, *Christus Dominus,* in mandating a General Directory, had already dealt with the ques-tion. Pope Paul VI, communicating through Cardinal Jean Villot, then prefect of the Congregation for the Clergy, reaffirmed his support for a General Catechetical Directory.

The *Directorium catechisticum generale,* after a protracted con-sultation with episcopal conferences, appeared in the summer of 1971. Part I sketches some of the factors, including social change and cultural pluralism, that affect the church's mission to pro-claim the gospel in the modern world. Part II relates catechesis to revelation and evangelization, and describes its nature and goals in the context of the church's pastoral mission. Part III gives spe-cific norms for the presentation of the Christian message, and outlines its "more outstanding elements." (This outline was assim-ilated almost immediately in the U.S. document *Basic Teachings of Catholic Religious Education,* then in progress of being written.) Part IV discusses the strengths and limitations of various methods used in catechesis, stressing the importance of formulas (n. 73) and

experience (n. 74). Part V gives guidelines for catechesis according to the special needs of various age levels. Part VI is concerned
with practical matters such as the formation of catechists, organization, and catechetical materials, including catechisms "published
by ecclesiastical authority" (n. 119).

In the mind of some, however, the Directory was not an adequate substitute for a catechism. The third general assembly of
the Synod of Bishops in 1974 had as its topic evangelization—"the
proclamation of the gospel to people of our time." That assembly
witnessed a degree of tension between those bishops who recognized the challenges presented by cultural differences and those
bishops who insisted on uniformity of doctrinal expression as a
means of insuring unity of faith. The latter favored a *catechismus
typicus* ("a paradigmatic catechism") as a necessary means to that
end, but they were in a minority. (It should be noted that the
Polish language group favored a catechism, and a member of that
group was the cardinal archbishop of Cracow, Karol Wojtyla.)
Pope Paul VI's Apostolic Exhortation *Evangelii nuntiandi* reflected
the stance of the majority of bishops when it stated,

> A means of evangelization that must not be neglected is that of
> catechetical instruction. The intelligence, especially that of chil-
> dren and young people, needs to learn through systematic re-
> ligious instruction the fundamental teachings, the living content
> of the truth which God has wished to convey. . . . Truly the ef-
> fort for evangelization will profit greatly—at the level of cate-
> chetical instruction given at church, in schools, where this is
> possible, and in every case in Christian homes—if those giving
> catechetical instruction have suitable texts, updated with wis-
> dom and competence, under the authority of the bishops. The
> methods must be adapted to the age, culture and aptitude of
> the persons concerned . . . (n. 44).

The Synod on Evangelization touched on many aspects of catechesis, but the fourth general assembly of the Synod of Bishops in
1977 addressed them directly. The theme, "catechesis in our time,
especially for children and youth," provided a context for a discussion of every facet of catechesis and related issues. It should
not come as a surprise that it was an occasion for overt lobbying
on the part of individuals who linked what they perceived as a "cri-

sis in the church" to the direction of catechesis in the post-Vatican II years. When the bishops arrived in Rome, they became aware that organized cliques, including an American group, had complained to Paul VI and the synod fathers that their bishops were not doing enough to safeguard the integrity of the Christian message.[3]

Although the issue of catechisms was not mentioned in the outline of themes proposed for discussion at the synod (*Lineamenta*) or the "Working Paper" (*Instrumentum laboris*) that set the agenda, it surfaced in interventions made by bishops from the floor. There was little agreement, however, in the kind of catechism envisioned by the bishops. Some expressed the desire for a short catechism that could serve as a fundamental text of Christian doctrine for youngsters; some called for a catechism that would be a compilation of the teachings of Vatican II; a few spoke of a catechism to guide catechists; and five proposed a catechism that would be normative for the universal church. The differences became more obvious in the discussion groups (*circuli minores*). Eight of the eleven groups that took up the issue of the catechism were divided on the question, and it was evident that the bishops were far from a consensus with regard to both the contents and the utility of a catechism for the universal church. (Cardinal Pericle Felici, head of the Commission for the Revision of the Code of Canon Law, stated that a new catechism was unnecessary because the church already has a list of normative beliefs in Pope Paul VI's *Credo of the People of God*.) In the end, the synod made no recommendation as regard to a catechism.

In his closing address to the synod, Pope Paul commented on several of the synod's recommendations. The pope said that he took comfort in the emphasis that the synod put on "systematic catechesis" because "this orderly study of the Christian mystery is what distinguishes catechesis itself from all other forms of presentation of the word of God." He also endorsed the synod's insistence on the need for "some fundamental formulas which will make it possible to express more easily, in a suitable and accurate way, the truths of the faith and of Christian moral doctrine." He said that such formulas—among which he cited important biblical texts and liturgical texts that serve to express common prayer—"if learned by heart," greatly aid the stable possession of these truths and make the profession of faith easier.[4]

Paul VI was at work on an apostolic exhortation addressing issues raised by the synod when he died, and it was left to Pope John Paul II to complete it. In the Introduction to *Catechesi tradendae* John Paul notes that he had participated in the 1977 synod and that "Catechesis has always been a central care in my ministry as a priest and as a bishop" (nn. 2, 4). This is not the occasion to attempt an analysis of *Catechesi tradendae*, the most comprehensive statement on the catechetical ministry in the church's annals, but I want to single out certain passages that set the context for the *Catechism of the Catholic Church* and help explain its contents and structure.[5]

*Catechesi tradendae* returns to Pope Paul's emphasis on systematic catechesis. Without denigrating the need for catechesis for personal, family, social, and ecclesial life, Pope John Paul writes, "I am stressing the need for organic and systematic Christian instruction, because of the tendency in various quarters to minimize its importance" (n. 21). The handing over of the Creed—the *traditio symboli*—along with the Lord's Prayer in the initiation of catechumens deserves a prominent place in catechesis. Pope John Paul declares that the Creed of the People of God "is a sure point of reference for the content of catechesis" because it brings together the essential elements of the Catholic faith, especially those that present major difficulty or risk being ignored (n. 28). *Catechesi tradendae* picks up a theme that ran through the 1977 synod, namely that the Christian faith be presented in its entirety and that catechists on their own initiative cannot decide what is important and unimportant "so as to teach the one and neglect the other" (n. 30).

Part VI of *Catechesi tradendae* describes various "ways and means of catechesis," including electronic media, special occasions, the homily, and textbooks and other catechetical materials. In this context John Paul makes reference to catechisms. They must take "their inspiration from the General Catechetical Directory," which, he says, "remains the standard of reference." And then the pope continues,

> In this regard, I must warmly encourage the episcopal conferences of the whole world to undertake, patiently but resolutely, the considerable work to be accomplished in agreement with the Apostolic See in order to prepare genuine catechisms which will be faithful to the essential content of revelation and up to

date in method, and which will be capable of educating the Christian generations of the future to a sturdy faith (n. 50).

*Catechesi tradendae* is dated October 16, 1979—fifteen years after the close of Vatican II. Given the lukewarm support that a catechism for the universal church had received in the commissions that prepared for the Second Vatican Council, in the council itself, and in the general assemblies of the Synod of Bishops, there was no indication that a catechism for the universal church was on the horizon. In retrospect, the only hint one finds that the idea still had life is a paragraph of *Catechesi tradendae*:

> The ministry of catechesis draws ever fresh energy from the councils. The Council of Trent is a noteworthy example of this. It gave catechesis priority in its constitutions and decrees. It lies at the origin of the Roman Catechism, which . . . is a work of the first rank as a summary of the Christian teaching and traditional theology for use by priests. It gave rise to a remarkable organization of catechesis in the church. It aroused the clergy to their duty of giving catechetical instruction. Thanks to the work of holy theologians such as St. Charles Borromeo, St. Robert Bellarmine and St. Peter Canisius, it involved the publication of catechisms that were real models for that period. May the Second Vatican Council stir up in our time a like enthusiasm and similar activity (n. 13).

In light of subsequent events, the paragraph outlines the scenario for the preparation of the *Catechism of the Catholic Church,* and in fact it was cited in the provisional text in 1989 when the working-title was still a *Catechism for the Universal Church.*

## CONTROVERSY OVER CATECHISMS

The lingering question remains: Why did it take until 1985 before steps were taken to follow up on what seems a transparent invitation in *Catechesi tradendae* to produce a catechism along the lines of the Council of Trent? Certainly one answer lies in the people involved. Although Pope John Paul II invited to the Extraordinary Synod of 1985 a number of bishops, like Cardinals Dearden and Suenens, who had been leaders at Vatican II, it was evident that there had been a changing of the guard. A new generation had come into positions of leadership. But there was also a continuing preoccupation with a "crisis in the church," real or perceived, that was (is?) attributed in large part to disarray in the ranks of religious educators.

The drafting of the General Catechetical Directory, as we have noted, became the task of the Congregation of the Clergy, but before it was completed a new chapter in the history of catechisms had begun. In 1966 the Dutch bishops, encouraged by the council's emphasis on adult catechesis, had published *De Nieuwe Katechismus*. "We hope," they wrote in the Foreword, "to present anew to adults the message which Jesus of Nazareth brought into the world, to make it sound as new as it is . . . in a form suitable to the present day." The authors of the Dutch Catechism addressed questions of the day, sought to promote unity among Christians and to reach out to everyone who lives "in the same world as we do with all its cares and yearnings." The negative reaction of traditionalists, who held the attempts at the *aggiornamento* of Vatican II suspect, or who had little sympathy for the ecumenical movement or denigrated the challenges of contemporary culture, was understandable.

The brouhaha that surrounded the Dutch Catechism was not an isolated incident. In the United States opposition to the works of Gabriel Moran and to the catch-phrase "continuing revelation" cloaked resistance to new approaches to biblical studies, liturgical change, and ecumenical dialogue, and reflected nostalgia for the simple world of the Baltimore Catechism. In Germany, Hubertus Halbfas caused a stir with the publication of *Fundamentalkatechetick* (1968), in which he questioned the manner of presenting doctrine and challenged the basic structures and goals of German Catholic education. In Italy the cardinal archbishop of Florence banned the "Isolotto Catechism" because he felt that it presented Christ as a social agitator and reduced salvation to a liberation from oppression and exploitation. In France the bishops, exploring a novel approach to catechesis for children, authorized "a Catholic collection of privileged documents of the faith" that incorporated the scriptures, the Creed, liturgy, traditional prayers, church history, and contemporary witnesses to the faith. Because *Pierres Vivantes* was an official publication of the French hierarchy, it came under review by the Congregation for the Doctrine of the Faith, which directed that a number of changes be made. A year later, in 1984, Cardinal Joseph Ratzinger, prefect of the CDF, asked Archbishop Gerety of Newark to withdraw the *nihil obstat* and *imprimatur* from Anthony Wilhelm's best-selling *Christ Among Us*. The church in Argentina was divided over the use of *Hoja de Ruta*, a catechetical text that dealt with a variety of social issues of concern to youth. The cardinal archbishop of Buenos Aires objected to its use despite the fact that it had been developed under the aegis of the Salesian Catechetical Center and carried the *imprimatur* of the bishop of Quilmes.[6]

The controversies over *Pierres Vivantes* and *Christ Among Us* were already smoldering when Cardinal Ratzinger became prefect of the Congregation for the Doctrine of the Faith late in 1982. Cardinal Ratzinger's interest in catechisms pre-dates his appointment to the CDF. His critique of the Dutch Catechism in 1968 was widely circulated, and he played an important role in the production of the *Katholischer Erwachsenen-Katechismus* commissioned by the German bishops. (The title of the English translation is *A Catholic Adult Catechism*, Ignatius Press, 1987.) In January 1983 he gave a well-publicized lecture in France in which he said, "It was an initial and grave error to suppress the catechism and to declare obsolete the whole idea of catechisms." The abandonment of the catechism, he said, has contributed to the fragmentation of the proclamation of the Christian message, a certain arbitrariness in the way faith is explained, and a calling into question of some of its parts. He held up the Catechism of the Council of Trent, built around the four pillars of catechesis—creed, sacraments, commandments, and the Lord's Prayer—as the model catechism.[7]

Cardinal Ratzinger's remarks were either disingenuous or misunderstood because he knew that the idea of catechisms was neither suppressed nor obsolete. The publication of the Dutch Catechism, whatever must be said of the text itself, had given the genre new life. Even while work was going forward on the General Catechetical Directory, the Italian Episcopal Conference was carefully laying the groundwork for a new national catechism that was all but complete and in wide use by 1983. In 1981, Cardinal Ratzinger, then archbishop of Munich and chairman of the Commission for the Faith of the German Episcopal Conference, himself had enlisted

Walter Kasper of the Catholic Faculty at the University of Tübingen to draft the text of a new catechism for adults—the *Katholischer Erwachsenen-Katechismus* mentioned above. In an address to the German Episcopal Conference in the spring of 1984, a few months before the new catechism appeared, Kasper described its development and situated it in the history of catechesis. Kasper acknowledged that the Catechism of the Council of Trent established the paradigm of Catholic catechisms, and he conceded that he had also been influenced by more immediate precedents: the Dutch Catechism; the ecumenical *Neues Glaubensbuch,* published in English as the *Common Catechism* (Herder, 1975); and the adult catechism published by the Evangelical (Lutheran) Church in 1975.[8] (It might also be added that Kasper wrote a position paper to help the German bishops prepare for the Extraordinary Assembly of the Synod in 1985 in which he spoke of a "crisis" or "collapse" in catechetics.)[9]

## A POINT OF REFERENCE AND GUIDING PRINCIPLES

Professor Kasper made it clear that the compilation of a catechism is a complex task. Despite the fact that the Tridentine Catechism provides a model for the *Catechism of the Catholic Church,* there was no ready-made recipe for adapting the genre to the needs of the twentieth century. It is interesting to notice, for example, how Cardinal Law's original proposal evolved within days after he first made it in the *aula* of the Extraordinary Synod. Cardinal Law called for

> a Commission of Cardinals to prepare a draft of a Conciliar Catechism to be promulgated by the Holy Father after consulting the bishops of the world. In a shrinking world—a global village—national catechisms will not fill the current need for clear articulation of the church's faith.

When Pope John Paul II acknowledged the formal recommendation of the synod, he envisaged

> a catechism or compendium of all Catholic doctrine regarding both faith and morals . . . a point of reference for the catechisms or compendiums that are prepared in the various

regions. The presentation of doctrine must be biblical and liturgical. It must be sound doctrine suited to the present life of
Christians.

Whatever Cardinal Law thought about the relationship of a
"conciliar catechism" to national catechisms, Pope John Paul was
clear. In the spirit of Vatican II and the assemblies of the Synod of
Bishops, the pope saw the new Catechism as a means of enhanc-
ing, but not replacing, regional and national catechisms. As work
went forward and in the course of the consultation with the bishops of the world, the focus of the Catechism was sharpened. Toward the end of their work, the Commission of the Catechism of
the Catholic Church published an "informative dossier" that explains the main principles that guided their work.[10] First, it speaks
of the Catechism "as an instrument to convey the essential and
fundamental content of Catholic faith and moral teaching in a complete and summary way—*non omnia sed totum*. The commission reaffirmed that the Catechism is a reference tool for national and
diocesan catechisms "whose mediation is indispensable." The Catechism is intended to be a positive and objective presentation of
Catholic teaching. It is not a "small catechism" for use by children
and youth, but belongs to the genre of the *catechismus major*, that
is, catechisms "meant for promoters and teachers of catechesis."
Later the dossier is more specific in identifying the readers for whom
the Catechism is intended. "The *Catechism of the Catholic Church* is
addressed first and foremost to the bishops, insofar as they are the
doctors of the faith, then to the compilers of catechisms, and,
through them, to all the people of God."

The dossier goes on to say that the Catechism "is characterized
by its concerns for essentials, its conciseness, sobriety, incisiveness
and clarity." It leaves the task of adapting the Catechism to the socio-
cultural and ecclesial circumstances of particular countries to
national catechisms. Pedagogical methods and strategies are also
left to national and diocesan catechisms. The dossier describes
the Catechism's style as "declarative" rather than apologetic, and
says that it aims "at proclaiming the Christian truth with the certainty
proper to the church . . . [while avoiding] theological opinions."

The dossier is also clear that the Catechism "cannot be called
the 'Catechism of the Second Vatican Council,' since it was not man-

dated by the council." Although the *Catechism of the Catholic Church* is "dedicated to the full and faithful expression and implementation of the teaching" of Vatican II, it draws its contents from other sources than the council. My task is not to analyze these contents—I leave that to others. I have focused more on the formal structure and purpose of the *Catechism of the Catholic Church* than on its contents.

From Pope John Paul himself and the commission of cardinals that he appointed to set the parameters of the work, to the editorial commission responsible for the text of the Catechism, there has been an effort to remain faithful to the spirit of Vatican II. Before, during, and after the council, many who favored a catechism for the universal church saw it as condemning errors and correcting questionable theological opinions. Undoubtedly that is one of the reasons that the early proposals for a catechism got so little support. Pope John Paul set the agenda when he affirmed that the Catechism's "presentation of doctrine should be biblical and liturgical, presenting sure teaching adapted to the actual life of Christians." The editorial commission made a conscious effort to link catechesis to evangelization, emphasizing throughout the central nucleus of the Christian proclamation, namely, God's plan of salvation realized in Christ. The authors of the catechism were sensitive to ecumenical concerns, and sought to reflect the open and constructive dialogue with non-Christian religions found in *Nostra aetate* of Vatican II.

## THE TASK AHEAD

At no point does the *Catechism of the Catholic Church* repudiate the efforts of the modern catechetical movement. In the Apostolic Constitution *Fidei depositum* that prefaces the Catechism, Pope John Paul writes,

> This *Catechism* is not intended to replace the local catechisms duly approved by the ecclesiastical authorities, the diocesan bishops and episcopal conferences, especially those that have received the approval of the Apostolic See. It is intended to encourage and assist in the writing of new local catechisms which take into account the different situations and cultures but which

carefully guard the unity of the faith and fidelity to Catholic doctrine (n. 4).[11]

If there is any doubt as to Pope John Paul's meaning, Cardinal Jose Sanchez, the prefect of the Congregation of the Clergy, which has the responsibility "of setting guidelines to direct the right mediation and inculturation of the *Catechism of the Catholic Church*," says that the Catechism "is not intended as a substitute for local, duly approved catechisms." In an article that appeared in the April 14, 1993 English edition of *L'Osservatore Romano*, Cardinal Sanchez says that it is a mistake to think that there is no longer any need for local catechisms and catechetical works.

Cardinal Sanchez acknowledges that the sheer size and theological depth of the Catechism precludes using it as "the basic textbook for catechists, especially at the primary level." On the other hand, he cautions against simply relying on the summaries at the end of each section, the "in brief" statements, as a basic text. It may be necessary, however, to take this approach "in countries where catechetical structures are not developed to the point of producing local catechisms, and also in catechetically developed countries where it is impossible to produce national catechisms because of great social and cultural disparity among the various regions."

In Cardinal Sanchez' mind the publication of the *Catechism of the Catholic Church* marks a new beginning. He seems to approve the notion that the Catechism presents "the unique and essential content," namely, Catholic doctrine, "while leaving to catechists and their catechetical materials (not to catechisms) the task of inculturating and incarnating the message." With the publication of the *Catechism of the Catholic Church*, we have an authoritative, reliable *regula fidei*; but the Catechism leaves to catechists the task of making the faith come alive in the hearts and minds of individuals.

# THE AUTHORITY OF THE CATECHISM

## Joseph A. Komonchak

Questions about the authority of doctrinal texts of the church's magisterium are often posed simply in terms of their juridical authority, that is, the degree to which a teaching is "binding" on the consciences of the faithful or, correspondingly, the level of assent that believers are obliged to give. Positively, this approach reflects a legitimate concern, first, for the integrity of the faith and its expression—common meaning and value being a key element of the communion that constitutes the church as first of all a *congregatio fidelium*—second, for the various degrees to which the church is committed to certain teachings, and, third, for the freedom of the Christian conscience. As the popular phrase, often quoted by Pope John XXIII, put it: "Unity in necessary things, freedom in doubtful things, love in all things." The Code of Canon Law respects these differentiations in its canons on the Church's teaching role,[1] and the recent instruction of the Congregation for the Doctrine of the Faith, "On the Ecclesial Vocation of the Theologian," went into some detail in confirming and explaining the differences in levels of magisterial teaching and expected responses.[2]

Along with the positive side of this approach to official texts, there are certain disadvantages that at times accompany it. First, it tends to reduce the communication of the church's faith to acts of the church's formal and official teaching office. This neglects the hosts of other ways in which the church hands on the faith from generation to generation: preaching, catechesis, witness, liturgy, the example of holy lives, etc. A second temptation is to regard teaching itself as a species of legislation, with the related reduction of assent to obedience.[3] A third problem is the tendency to pulverize the organic unity of the Christian message into hundreds or thousands of individual statements about which one's first concern is to determine the formal authority that lies behind them. Whether on the part of defenders of church authority or among the defenders of a right to dissent, this can lead to a neglect of the material authority of the Christian gospel—its integrative, synthetic, and persuasive force—giving more weight to extrinsic motives of faith and communion than to the help of the Holy Spirit, without whom "no one can say 'Jesus is Lord'" (1 Cor 12:3). In moments of ecclesial tension, this often results by reaction in a "Show me" attitude that is the opposite of the relationship of trust that in fact ought to mark the existence and exercise of authority in any social body, but particularly in the church.

One would like to hope, then, that in discussing the doctrinal authority of the new *Catechism of the Catholic Church,* we will be able to go beyond the tendency of those who might wish to turn the 2,865 paragraphs in this Catechism into so many binding propositions and of those who might approach it distrustfully—wondering what's wrong with it—and therefore ask only what legal weight lies behind individual sections or statements.

## JOHN PAUL II FORMALLY PROMULGATES THE CATECHISM

For a judgment on the doctrinal authority of the *Catechism of the Catholic Church,* one turns first to the Apostolic Constitution, *Fidei depositum,* with which Pope John Paul II ordered its publication on October 11, 1992.[4] An apostolic constitution is the most solemn form with which popes promulgate official church documents, and has been used since the council, for example, for the promulgation of the revised Roman Missal and other rites, for the new Codes of Canon Law, for the reform of the Roman curia, etc.

The words of formal authorization are found in the fourth section of *Fidei depositum,* under the sub-title "The Doctrinal Value of the Text":

> The Catechism of the Catholic Church, which I approved last June 25 and *the publication of which I today order by virtue of my apostolic authority,* is a statement of the church's faith and of Catholic doctrine, attested to or illumined by sacred scripture, apostolic tradition and the church's magisterium. I declare it

to be a valid and legitimate instrument in the service of ecclesial communion and a sure norm for the teaching of the faith. May it serve the renewal to which the Holy Spirit ceaselessly calls the church of God, the body of Christ, on its pilgrimage to the unshadowed light of the Kingdom!

The pope went on to say that he offered his approval of the Catechism as a service to the whole church and all the particular churches in fulfillment of his Petrine service of "supporting and confirming the faith of all the Lord Jesus' disciples (see Lk 22:32) as well as of strengthening the bonds of unity in the same apostolic faith." He then stated what he wished to see as a response to this service: "Therefore, I ask the church's pastors and the Christian faithful to receive this Catechism in a spirit of communion and to use it assiduously in fulfilling their mission of proclaiming the faith and calling people to the life of the gospel." It was given as "a sure and authentic reference text" for teaching Catholic doctrine and particularly for preparing local catechisms. If it is not intended to replace duly authorized catechisms already in use, "it is meant to encourage and assist in the writing of new local catechisms, which must take into account various situations and cultures, while carefully preserving the unity of faith and fidelity to Catholic doctrine."

What is striking in this section is the absence of such solemn juridical language as is usually found in documents with immediate legal consequences. The words of formal approval occur in a subordinate clause. The pope formally declares or, as the French and Italian texts put it, "recognizes," the Catechism to be a "sure norm for teaching the faith"; and because it is "a sure and authentic reference text," he "asks" bishops and the faithful to make assiduous use of it as they undertake their tasks of catechizing, in particular the preparation of local catechisms. The language is the language of communion; his act of approval is an exercise of the Petrine ministry within the universal communion of the churches; and the pastors and other faithful of the particular churches are invited to make it their own.

While the approval of the Catechism was a papal act, the pope in an earlier section noted that its preparation had had a collegial character. Wide consultation had been made and the episcopate had been "broadly favorable"; the Catechism thus is "the result of a collaboration of the whole episcopate." It could thus be said to "reflect the collegial nature of the episcopate; it testifies to the church's catholicity." The pope's careful language here reflects the process of the Catechism's preparation, which did involve a certain participation of the bishops in the proposal of such a Catechism and in the evaluation of a draft text, although not in its final stages nor in the act of approval.[5] While, therefore, the process was collegial to a certain degree, it cannot be said to represent the sort of full collegiality that lies behind the documents that are written, debated, revised, agreed upon, and promulgated in the course of an ecumenical council.

It is clear from the language of Pope John Paul II, both in speaking of the collaboration of the bishops and in the words of formal approval, that the Catechism as such is not to be ranked among the supreme and most solemn forms of church teaching: dogmatic definitions of a pope or of an ecumenical council. The pope's words and the character of the collegial consultation would also seem to place the Catechism as a whole at a level below that of the documents of the Second Vatican Council.

## "A SURE NORM FOR THE TEACHING OF THE FAITH"

After these negative judgments, it becomes more difficult to describe the formal authority of the Catechism. Its publication obviously represents an exercise of the ordinary teaching authority of the church, and, immediately, of the bishop of Rome.[6] He has placed his apostolic authority behind it as "a sure norm for the teaching of the faith," "a sure and authentic reference text." This means that it can be trusted and should be welcomed for the guidance it can supply to those, bishops and other faithful, who assume the tasks of concrete catechesis in local churches.

The literary genre of the text must also be taken into account. Here the first difficulty is that we lack clear parallels. "Reference text" is, as far as I know, a new category of magisterial documents. (I will attempt an explanation of this term later.) Popes have approved catechisms in the past, most notably the "Catechism of the Council of Trent," the influence of which on subsequent catechesis was great perhaps more because of the considerable merits of that text than because it was considered, strictly speaking, an exercise of the magisterium.[7] (It was never included in collections of magisterial texts such as Denziger's *Enchiridion.*)

Secondly, as Cardinal Ratzinger has pointed out, the Catechism tries to present the faith positively and serenely and not argumentatively or apologetically.[8] It is intended to be a model of how to give a confident expression of what the Catholic Church believes, of what it celebrates, of what it tries to live, of what it prays for. It is in the genre of an authoritative witness and should be read and evaluated as such.

Similarly, as Bishop Christoph Schönborn, secretary of the commission that drafted the new catechism, remarked, it is intended to provide "an organic, complete and synthetic exposition of the Christian faith."[9] As such, of course, it contains elements that belong to the central core of the church's faith and elements that are, by comparison, secondary or derivative. Schönborn also stated the criterion for determining this "hierarchy of truths": "The dogmatic value of the different elements that constitute a catechism depends on the proximity of such or such an affirmation to the center of our faith. This center is the affirmation of the mystery of the Most Holy Trinity, the mystery of Christ, of the Holy Spirit and of the church."

Here, of course, is where a certain difficulty arises. The drafting commission said that the Catechism concentrates on "essentials," on only "those elements that are recognized as universally valid," while also respecting "the different levels of certainty which the church has of the several themes" and avoiding "theological opinions." Similarly, Cardinal Ratzinger maintains, on the one hand, that the Catechism "wishes to present the essential and basic contents of Christian faith and morality," but, on the other, that it was a constant concern of the drafters

> to distinguish, in presenting the various and complementary Christian themes, what is basic, essential, immutable from what is secondary, transitory, peripheral . . . to respect and to show the different links and references of Christian truths to their center, which is Christ (the "hierarchy of truths"), on the one hand indicating the proximity of each truth to the central nucleus of the faith and thus the interdependence and inter-

connection of each truth and, on the other, respecting the various "levels of certainty" of the truths.[10]

The Catechism, in other words, contains matters that have been the object of solemn dogmatic definition and others that have been handed down or officially taught with a much inferior formal authority. The legitimacy of a criterion of formal authority is here implicitly acknowledged, although, of course, it must be used carefully, since there are central doctrines of Christian faith that have never been the object of dogmatic definition. Bishop Schönborn is correct, then, when he warns against equating the hierarchy of truths with the levels of certainty.[11] On the other hand, the Catechism does not supply much help in distinguishing among the various "levels of certainty" with which it presents its teachings.[12] Clearly, then, in assessing the degree to which the church has committed itself to particular doctrines, the classical norms of theological interpretation will have to be invoked: the character and authority of the sources from which the doctrines are drawn, the frequency and universality with which they are taught, the style of the texts in which they are proposed, etc. Inclusion of various elements in the new Catechism will not by itself settle the issue of the varying degrees of authority that lie behind them.[13]

Similar observations must be made about another comment of Cardinal Ratzinger: that the drafters also tried "as much as possible to avoid theological opinions, both by not preferring one or another particular theological synthesis and by not 'closing' particular questions that remain open and that are the object of theological research and reflection."[14] As his clause ("as much as possible") indicates, this is a very difficult, perhaps an impossible, task, and the success of the drafters in accomplishing it is likely also to be a matter of theological discussion.

## THE "SUMMARY FORMULAS"—NUCLEUS OF FAITH?

In this connection, perhaps something should be said about the summary statements ("In Brief") that appear after each section, which some may be tempted to regard as new and authoritative, if not dogmatic, formulas. Here Cardinal Ratzinger's comments are again helpful, both to understand their purpose and to identify the problem they can represent. He describes them as "synthetic propositions which summarize in simple and essential form themes of a certain importance," enucleations of "the basic and essential content of Christian truths as over the centuries it has been gradually adapted and explicated in the pluriform churches, liturgies, theologies, and personalities of faith." These statements are designed to help identify the essential "nucleus of faith" and "the basic traits of Christian identity"; they are "models of a summary exposition of the faith." While such formulas are thought to be aids to memorization, an indispensable part of the whole process of catechesis, they remain "strictly linked to the corresponding paragraphs which illustrate their correct meaning."

The use of these formulas in catechesis, according to the cardinal, reflects the two dimensions of the Catechism: it is at once intended for the whole church and yet requires transposition into local catechisms. On the one hand, particular care for "conceptual and terminological precision" was taken in the preparation of the formulas, and they were designed to promote "the acquisition of a common language of faith that would respect both the unrenounceable patrimony of the past and the catholic and therefore transcultural dimension of Christian faith as well as the specific characteristics of man as he stands at the threshold of the millennium." On the other hand, they are themselves "inculturated expressions of the faith" and will need to be "further and appropriately adapted," a work that will

> demand a further indispensable effort at inculturation at the local level, both adequately to respond to the psychological and pedagogical exigencies of those being addressed in the different cultural contexts and to make it easier for them to be memorized, a matter that very much depends also on the literary and morphological characteristics of the various languages.[15]

A few observations. First, the brief statements are a very mixed bag. Some of them are direct biblical citations; some are dogmatic definitions; some reproduce or paraphrase other kinds of magisterial statements; some reflect insights of past or present theologians; some are drawn from the church's prayer; some articulate central and essential dimensions of Christian faith or life; some express dimensions that are derivative; some are edifying exhortations; some are simple descriptions of church practice; etc. It is impossible to bring them all under a single rubric of the classical theological notes.

Second, their meaning and, it also seems, their authority are to be determined by reference to the earlier paragraphs, the sense of which they attempt, with greater or lesser success, to summarize. In other words, the brief statements are to be interpreted in the light of the corresponding paragraphs and not vice versa. Finally, they will need to be adapted in order to serve their purpose in the varied contexts in which catechesis is undertaken by local churches.

For all these reasons, it would be a mistake to isolate the summary statements from their larger hermeneutical context and to use them as the sole or even the principal expression of the Catechism's teachings.

## THE CATECHISM AS A "REFERENCE-TEXT" AND ITS RECEPTION BY THE LOCAL CHURCHES

After discussing some of the issues involved in determining the formal authority of the Catechism, some attention should be given to the term "reference text" as a designation of the Catechism's status. Pope John Paul II makes clear, on the one hand, that it is not intended to displace already approved catechisms and, on the other hand, that it is meant to assist and encourage the writing of local catechisms. The *Catechism of the Catholic Church*, in other words, is not an end in itself. While it may be of great value and use to all Catholics, to ecumenists, and to interested non-Catholics, its drafters were quite conscious that the Catechism itself requires, as an indispensable complement, that local and particular churches fulfill their responsibility and exercise their right to carry out the task of concrete catechesis in their own cultural contexts.

Cardinal Ratzinger has been particularly insistent on this "indispensable condition" if the Catechism itself is "to be able fully to actuate its nature and completely to realize its objectives." On it, he says, depends in great measure "not only the proper use, but even the success itself and the desired fruits of the *Catechism of the*

*Catholic Church.*"[16] This is surely one of the clearest recognitions ever given of the necessity and validity of the process of "reception" of magisterial texts.

The whole project of the Catechism is thus inserted into one of the most dramatic developments in the post-conciliar church, the growing recognition that the one church only exists, lives, and accomplishes its mission in the many local and particular churches. The proposal of a universal catechism, the work which has resulted from it, and the reception it will likely receive in the years ahead reflect the tensions that characterize this development within a church that for many centuries was marked by a growing centralization and uniformity.

Some people welcomed the project of a universal catechism both as a safeguard against threats to the one church's unity of faith and as a response to an increasingly unitary world-culture. Others opposed it out of fears that it would impose a single text to be used everywhere and would thus represent an intolerable limit on the necessity of genuinely inculturated catechesis. It is likely that one's anticipation of the catechism project, as expressed in these viewpoints, will largely determine how a person responds to the new Catechism.

The issues at stake and the way in which the Catechism attempts to address them are well illustrated in Cardinal Ratzinger's comments. The central question is posed by the fact that the one universal church is only realized in the many local churches. Addressed to the universal church, the Catechism could not adequately express "the peculiar characteristics, the distinct exigencies, the specific problematics of the pluriform local churches." While the contribution of bishops and others from all over the world assured attention to the universal context in which the church lives today, the Catechism had to be limited "to those basic, general, essential aspects that today as always distinguish the church in its being and action in the various parts of the world and to some particular aspects that are frequently enough found in the pluriform local churches."

But if there are elements that distinguish the church across times and cultures and some aspects that define the situations of many or even most of the churches today, and if it is these that directed the preparation of the Catechism, other aspects of the concrete realization of the one church in the many churches need to be addressed by local catechisms. Theirs is "the task of giving voice to the multiple gifts that, sometimes in specific ways, enrich the various churches, welcoming, developing, and completing what belongs to the distinct character and traditions of the particular churches whose language they use, whose socio-cultural ecclesial characteristics they respect, whose exigencies they interpret." The relation between the *Catechism of the Catholic Church* and the local catechisms, then, reflects that "sort of osmosis" that exists between the universal church and the particular churches.[17]

## THE "INDISPENSABLE ROLE OF LOCAL CATECHISMS"

Cardinal Ratzinger addressed the doctrinal issue involved in distinguishing the doctrine of faith and its expression. On the one hand, "the basic and essential content of the Christian message is always the same: yesterday, today, and tomorrow, here, there, and everywhere." On the other hand, "this truth, while remaining ever the same, whole, and immutable, admits and even of its nature demands variety and diversity in its cultural clothing, in its modes of understanding and expression, in accordance with places, times, cultures and persons."[18]

This explains "the importance, the indispensable role of local catechisms," whose tasks the cardinal describes in a remarkable list:

> Making the content of catechesis more intelligible, while respecting the organic and hierarchical character of Christian truths; deepening and broadening the themes only sketched; expressing them in a language more fitted to the times and more close to the integral richness of the faith; proclaiming the assertions of faith in a way that is more faithful and more attentive to the exigencies, the expectations, and the problematics of those being addressed: these are only some of the tasks that await those who undertake the work of catechetical proclamation, in their indispensable work of inculturating the faith in general and the *Catechism of the Catholic Church* in particular.[19]

All this helps one understand what it means for the Catechism to be a reference text for this effort. Ratzinger presents it as itself an example of an "inculturated catechetical model" in the post-conciliar church and in the contemporary world on the eve of the third millennium. The effort to make a statement of the Christian faith and its publication under the authority of the ordinary magisterium of the pope responds to "certain characteristic problematics of the world today: a selective subjectivism, the splintering into different messages, the collapse of human certainties and systems, the process of secularization with the eclipse of the sacred and the irrelevance of the religious."

The Catechism, in other words, is a model of the effort to restate the Christian message in the face of contemporary challenges and needs. As intended for the whole church, it concentrates on what is basic and essential, not in some supra-temporal or supracultural sphere, but in response to certain cultural phenomena that its drafters consider to be particularly urgent and widespread in the world today. The preparation of the Catechism, then, is at once a defense of the traditional substance of the faith, interpreted in terms of its redemptive relevance to our age. In the cardinal's words,

> it is offered as an example of fidelity to the integral and original richness of the Christian mystery, whose essential and basic contents are re-expressed in a new form that maintains their integrity and completeness. In this way it offers an effective, although limited, contribution to that difficult and unceasing effort at the inculturation of the one and immutable truth of Christ that is the task of the whole church, but in particular of pastors, theologians, and catechists.[20]

As important and even necessary as was the task the drafters took upon themselves, the Catechism inevitably suffers from certain structural limitations, which the cardinal frankly acknowledged:

> Certainly, no expression, formulation, cultural mediation, and therefore not even the best catechism, has succeeded, is succeeding or will succeed in expressing adequately, thoroughly, exhaustively the richness, the depth, the breadth of the Christian mystery, considering the historical, social, cultural conditions of human understanding and expression of any age or place. For this reason we are well aware of the structural and contingent limits of this Catechism. . . . It is not and cannot be

considered the only possible way or the best way of giving a cat-echetical re-expression of the Christian message.

Nonetheless, despite such indisputable limits, the Catechism, insofar as it tries to express, truly and worthily, if always inade-quately, the essential and basic contents of Catholic faith and morality, has what it needs to present itself as a model, as a point of reference, as a beacon to illumine and to lead to new and safe harbors the unceasing and eager effort at the inculturation of faith and of catechesis.[21]

## A COMPARISON TO VATICAN II

In reflecting on and evaluating the project embodied in the new Catechism, it may be helpful to compare it to the effort under-taken at the Second Vatican Council. During the first session of the council, a vigorous debate took place over the pastoral orien-tation that Pope John XXIII had called for in his inaugural speech. Some bishops argued that the council's role was to issue dogmat-ic statements and that it would be the task of bishops and priests, later, to make pastoral "applications." Another group, the one that prevailed, argued that the council's presentation of the doc-trines of the church should itself always keep in mind the audience, the "modern world," to which it was addressed. Some bishops replied that in fact the pastoral audiences that the church addresses today are a very varied lot, that there are in fact many "worlds." How could the council, as an expression of the universal magisterium, be expected to speak in a pastoral way to all of them at once? In the end, of course, the council did produce sixteen documents that were meant for the whole church, including one that was even called a *pastoral* document, the "Pastoral Constitution on the Church in the Modern World."

But if Vatican II represented an example of an effort by the one church to declare its faith, the council had to be followed by the laborious task, still underway, of propagating its teachings into the lives of the different local churches, an effort that is not sim-ply a matter of deductivistic "applications." In the course of this process of reception certain features of the governing hermeneu-tics of the council became much clearer, particularly the fact that

by the "modern world" to which it addressed itself it meant largely the developed world of the west. Likewise, the reading of the
"signs of the times" that guided its pastoral orientation reflected
themes most pertinent to North Atlantic society and culture in the
early to mid-1960s. For churches in other circumstances (Latin
America, Africa, Asia, etc.) this posed the challenge of undertak-
ing themselves a task analogous to that of the council, of reread-
ing and restating the gospel message in the light of the challenges
and opportunities of their own times, places, and cultures.

The council itself then came to be seen, not as a single, uni-
formly relevant pastoral response to some supposedly single and
uniform "modern world," but as a reference point and model for
the permanently necessary task of presenting the Christian message in such a way as to reveal its manifold and varying redemptive
light and power. If Vatican II has been able to serve that purpose
and in this way to inspire and guide the lives of the local churches,
one can in principle hope that the new Catechism may also serve
a similar purpose and achieve a similar result. In fact, to judge
from their remarks, the principal drafters of the Catechism may
have had a keener sense than did the popes and bishops of Vatican II of the limits of their enterprise and of the hermeneutical and
ecclesial aspects involved.

## THE ONGOING PROCESS OF RECEPTION

Now that the Catechism has been completed, approved, and
translated, the process of its reception begins. Here, as with Vatican II, the key issue will be not only its formal authority but also its
material authority, that is, how well it has accomplished the purpose for which it was developed and what assistance it can provide
for local catechesis in the various local churches. The Catechism
should be judged on the basis of what the pope and its principal
drafters said when they described its character and limits, and not
on the basis of other agendas.

The new Catechism represents an effort, called for by many
bishops, supported by their collaboration, and formally approved
by Pope John Paul II in the exercise of his Petrine ministry, to offer a restatement of the Catholic faith in the late twentieth century. Its drafters were aware of and acknowledged, even if they do

not expressly identify, the varying degrees of certainty that mark its various statements. They offer it, not as an immediate tool for local catechesis, but as a source on which bishops and others can draw and as an example they can imitate as they assume their responsibility to do for their particular churches, in their quite varied social and cultural contexts and in the face of quite different challenges, what the Catechism has tried to do for the whole church. So far from forbidding local churches to undertake this task or of leading them to think that the task is exhausted by mere translation, it requires bishops and the other faithful to undertake a similar task of discernment, of interpretation, and of confident proclamation in and for their churches and their worlds.

We are thus led back to the invitation included when Pope John Paul II offered the Catechism: "I ask the church's pastors and the Christian faithful to receive this catechism in a spirit of communion and to use it assiduously in fulfilling their mission of proclaiming the faith and calling people to the life of the gospel."

# THE ROLE OF THE BIBLE IN CATECHESIS ACCORDING TO THE CATECHISM

## Gerard S. Sloyan

I did not feel completely at home in *Catéchisme de l'Eglise Catholique* (*Catechism of the Catholic Church*) until I reached numbered paragraph 1721. Its three and one-half lines begin: "For God has sent us into the world to know him, to serve him, and to love him and so come to paradise." That rang a bell as the answer to an early question in the catechism approved, although not yet compiled, by the Third Plenary Council of Baltimore in 1884 (published in 1885). Further assurance came with the list of sins "crying to heaven," although no longer "for vengeance," as in my youth. "The catechetical tradition [also] recalls to mind," says paragraph 1867, "that there exist 'sins that cry to heaven' . . . The blood of Abel; the sin of the men of Sodom; the outcry of the [people] oppressed in Egypt; the plaintive cry of the resident alien, the widow, and the orphan; and injustice to workers." I missed the sonorous "defrauding laborers of their just wages" from my childhood. Even more, I missed a footnote indicating that the "catechetical tradition" spoken of was the lists of seven of everything, as here, going back to the Carolingian era and, before that, to St. Isidore of Seville. There was, however, a biblical reference given for each of the seven sins, and two for injustice to wage-earners— one from Deuteronomy (24:14–15), the other from James (5:4).

That should provide a lead-in to my discussion of the role of the Bible in catechesis as this Catechism sees it. First, however, I should like to record a few other echoes raised by this volume "when mem'ries chains have bound me." In 1930, Pope Pius XI promulgated an encyclical letter on the Christian education of youth in which he proposed that there should be diocesan-wide contests in religious knowledge. In the Trenton diocese we were nothing if not docile, so we had a contest. I was in the eighth grade in 1932 and I won it. Three years later my sister Jean won it for seniors in the Catholic high schools of the diocese. Our present bishop of Trenton, an eighth grader that year, was one of our parish's two contestants. He did not win. John has a very good head but he was not yet of the *magisterium*, being fourteen at the time. The next year I was a senior and went off to South Amboy filled with spiritual pride—an imperfection in this case, not a grievous sin. Well, you know what "Pride goeth before . . ." Alas, I went down to ignominious defeat. My only memory was of a few matters that did not appear in the many European catechisms that Jean and I both swallowed whole, chiefly this: "What two English martyrs were canonized last year (1935) on the 400th anniversary of their deaths?" I had never heard of Fisher and More.

My point for the moment is that we were stuffed like Strassburg geese by our zealous teachers. We literally bulged with information about the nine choirs of angels and the properties of angelic being—incorporeality, incommensurability, agility, and subtility— likewise the seven ways to be accessory to another's sin, and the correlation of the seven gifts of the Holy Ghost with the beatitudes. That last required one to take the gifts to be seven with the Vulgate, and not six with the Hebrew, then reduce the Matthean beatitudes from nine or eight to seven and relate them to the gifts in reverse order.

I do not deride this knowledge. Much later in life I learned where it all came from. I only mention this because the Catechism under review often provides such incidental intelligence—though neither of those three examples—without the footnotes that cry to heaven for inclusion. There are ample citations in the Catechism from the Bible and from the fathers; some medievals—chiefly Aquinas but also a handful of mystics—church councils, some recent popes, and the 1983 Code of Canon Law. Often the status of a received tradition, such as the doctrine of purgatory or Jesus' descent into the netherworld, will be furnished with biblical texts that do not account for it or do so only by way of oblique illustration. Meanwhile, the historical development that explains how the doctrine came to be, which might have been encapsulated in a few well chosen sentences, does not appear.

We have in the Catechism a whole-earth catalogue—heaven,

too—largely of the faith and piety of Latin or western Christianity. It must be used with extreme care if catechetical materials for all Catholics—its stated purpose—are to be composed with its assistance. It speaks of the importance of the ecumenical formation of the faithful, and especially of priests (§ 821), but it provides none. Only when it quotes documents like the Pastoral Constitution on the Church in the Modern World, *Lumen Gentium,* or a modern papal letter on the social order like *Centesimus Annus* (1991) does it indicate that it knows the problems real people encounter in believing, worldwide. The Catechism does not seem to know of the existence of the Protestant churches, either the healthy developments within them or the threat that the doctrine of biblical inerrancy, sometimes called biblical literalism, poses to Catholic, Orthodox, and Protestant faith.

The volume is marvelously informative on some matters but woefully deficient in others; hence its use cries out at many points for nuance, supplementation, and correction. In the short run, adaptations of it should be attempted only by people who know as much theology or more than the authors. It cannot be promoted as a dependable book for use as it stands because of the uneven quality of its treatments. In brief, it requires a second, revised edition very soon. In the meantime, I strongly recommend recourse to the National Catechetical Directory for Catholics of the United States, *Sharing the Light of Faith* (1974) as a much more balanced performance.

## THE BIBLE IN THE CATECHISM: AN "ORACULAR SOURCE"?

Now to the role of the Bible in the Catechism. Two questions arise immediately. One is the book's catechesis *about* the Bible. The other is the way it uses the Bible itself, which gives many clues as to how it thinks the Bible should be used in catechizing.

As to the way the Bible is described as the church's book, only toward the end, § 2653 of 2863, are Catholics told that they should read the Bible. This occurs in the fourth and last part on prayer. But, since the invention of printing, the spread of literacy, and the availability of cheap Bibles, the fact that there is no strong charge to read the Bible is a gross omission. The problem is acute because

Catholics in every corner of the globe are being told that their faith is inauthentic: that only the Bible—the text of which they do not know—contains authentic faith. Apologetic considerations apart, Catholics need to know the Bible in itself if any extracts from it with which the Catechism teems are to be understood.

Nowhere is it made clear that a Bible text or texts can best be understood in context. That context is, first, the biblical book in which the passage occurs, and then the place of that book in the whole vast collection. A Matthean utterance of Jesus becomes meaningful to the believer who knows what Matthew's gospel is about; a Johannine soliloquy placed on Jesus' lips makes sense to one who knows the general tenor and techniques of John's gospel. So, too, with Leviticus and Job and Revelation and all the other biblical books.

The principles for interpreting the Bible given in *Dei Verbum* are listed early—the intentions of the authors, the conditions of their time and culture, the types of literature found there, and so on—but these are then conveniently forgotten. They are subordinated to the unity of the Bible as if all its books had the same purpose, and the reminder that the Holy Spirit brought it all about. That is the way the Bible is used throughout: as an oracular source that can justify whatever is previously known from doctrinal and ethical sources, rather than the other way about.

Although the literal sense of scripture—the obvious intent of the author in writing—is that on which all other senses must be based (Aquinas is quoted to this effect in § 116; Luther, who said the same with more telling effect, is not), the principle is not adhered to consistently. Occasionally, one of the three spiritual senses of the middle ages, cited in a limping translation of the once well-known Latin verse, will be resorted to: the *allegorical* for faith, the *moral* for conduct, and the *anagogic* for directing us to heaven. In Parts One and Two of the Catechism (on the creed and the sacraments), the patristic and medieval mode of citing the Bible—both Testaments indiscriminately—prevails, this whether the "literal" sense (what the biblical author was talking about) is at work or not. The citation practice of Parts Three and Four on Christian conduct and prayer is generally better.

In sum, the Catechism appears to be embarrassed by the study of the Bible in the west of the last two hundred years. Certain patristic insights into the possible uses of biblical texts are welcome. No one should expect a critical treatment of the scriptures in either catechesis or in homilies. But the post-enlightenment exploration of the book of the church has put all teachers and preachers on notice about what *not* to say about it, how *not* to use it. It has now become clear what the Bible does not mean in most of its passages—clearer, in fact, as in the books of the prophets, than what it does mean. The Catechism takes for granted, without spelling it out, that all its readers will be aware of the symbolic or figurative nature of much that is written there; that it is a book of words about the basically inexpressible; and that all its verbal symbols are interchangeable when the inexpressible requires expression. In the modern world the mentality about "truth" is so largely literal and so little symbolic that little is done for hearers of the Bible when this fact is disregarded. Sometimes the Bible takes the form of chronicle, often of laws or, again, of wise sayings. Rarely is it history in the modern sense. The Catechism's silences and the way its multiple citations are employed leave the impression that the Bible is largely history in the modern sense.

One example should suffice. Paragraph 339 points out that in Genesis 1 and 2 God's declaration at the end of each day of creation that the work was good shows the interdependence of all creatures, the beauty of the universe, and the hierarchy of creatures with the human creature at the summit. St. Francis of Assisi's *Canticle of the Sun* is quoted in a later paragraph. At the end of the treatment, we read in smaller print: "The creation was accomplished in view of the sabbath, therefore of the worship and adoration of God" (§ 347). But of course! To say this, however, and nothing more about the six-day scheme as an instructional device composed at a very late date is to leave Catholics open to attack from the "creationists" flourishing on every continent. Their belief in the way the creation was accomplished is quite different from that of the biblical authors' marvelous poem. It should be pointed out as a false reading of the text. In brief, in assuming that all Bible readers think like post-exilic Jews, this catechism never faces the problems that twentieth century Christians have with it. The cosmology taken for granted in the volume is roughly that of the third century Gentile Christians, who by that time had largely lost the Hebraic gift of symbolic speech.

One could not complain about the patristic-era use of the Bible that prevails if only the authors had made clear at some point how they were using it. Meanwhile, two important populations are left out of consideration: the simple, who are prey to the charge that Catholics do not believe exactly what the Bible says (as defined by those who make the charge) and the bright seventh grader in Zaire who already knows quite a lot about astrophysics. The half-sentence in § 283 acknowledging recent researches into cosmic origins simply does not do it.

To sum up, one often applauds where the Catechism begins in its use of the Bible texts but deplores the points at which it stops. It is as if some nervous censor were looking over its shoulder for signs of theological "liberalism" in its treatment of scriptural matters.

## THE BIBLE AND POST-BIBLICAL TRADITION

As to the writings that make up the Bible, § 120 lists the canon of the two testaments as the Council of Trent spelled it out in 1546 (Session 4, April 8; DS 1502–03). It does this without further comment. The Protestant tradition, of its very nature, had no way to compile an official list. It went with the Hebraist humanists of the time, who did not reckon six books and parts of Daniel and Esther as authentically biblical. The Greek-speaking east, for its part, had long opted for more books of the Septuagint than the Catholic west, although not all of them. It has never spelled out a canon, only adopted one by usage. A short paragraph could have made some of this clear. Meanwhile, Catholics will continue to hear that their canon of scripture contains apocryphal or spurious books that are not truly the word of God. If you think the present writer has an apologetic mentality that the Catechism lacks, be assured that he does. The volume goes on its serene way, convinced by and large that "there ain't nobody here but us Catholics." Meantime, our fellow communicants are under siege on biblical questions in every corner of the globe.

Paragraph 77 of Article 2, "The Transmission of the Divine Revelation," appositely quotes *Dei Verbum* 8: "Thus, the apostolic preaching, which is expressed in a special way in the inspired books, was to be preserved in a continuous line of succession until the end of time." In the next paragraph (78) the Catechism says in its own name: "This living transmission, accomplished in the Holy Spirit, is called Tradition [upper case] insofar as it is distinct from Holy Scripture, although strictly tied to it." (For this, see *Dei Verbum* 9.) There then follow some statements from this document, notably: "The sayings of the Holy Fathers are a witness to the life-giving presence of this Tradition." Now, the fact that the apostolic tradition is expressed in a special way in the inspired books is very important. Much should be made of it. There is nothing quite on a par with the twenty-seven New Testament books which, in turn, are interpretations of the Bible of the Jews, the very core of the primitive tradition. Together, the two collections testify to the apostolic tradition as nothing else does. This is true despite the fact that it took the church, acting as the inheritors of the tradition, about three hundred years to make a firm determination on which of its inspired books were canonical. In the meantime, teachings and practices were being testified to in other writings that continued to be thought of as inspired, if not canonical, up to the fifteenth century.

To take an example: the canonical scriptures contain no repudiation of abortion or infanticide but the second century *Didache, Pseudo-Barnabas,* and *Letter to Diognetus* all do, as a footnote to § 2271 duly observes. So far so good. This is a good example of extra-biblical church tradition, in this case inherited from Israel. But the early discussion of revelation does not make clear the absolute pre-eminence of the biblical witness to what was transmitted from the apostolic age. It never discusses the way that some teachings of the fathers constitute an authentic explication of the tradition and others do not. This is a complex question, not easily expounded, but it can be done. The Catechism goes about it in such a way as to create the impression that scripture and tradition are two sources of revelation rather than witnesses, of unequal importance, to the one apostolic tradition. This was the very thing *Dei Verbum* sought to express, whether it was successful in doing so or not.

Catholics go unarmed by this Catechism against the twofold charge that for them the Bible is not a unique divine deliverance, and that Catholics believe and do things not found in the Bible. There is no clear indication of how relatively recent the principle is that if a matter is not found in the scriptures (meaning the shorter canon of the first Testament) Christians have no warrant for it. In sum, biblical tradition is not sufficiently highlighted, while the way post-biblical tradition is related to the Bible is not sufficiently explained. This comes out glaringly when the Bible is quoted in support of belief in purgatory, indulgences, and the position of the bishopric of Rome. Catholic faith in these matters derives largely from a dynamic within the church's life. The biblical justification in each case was resorted to as the process developed.

This is not to say that the Catechism employs the Bible badly so much as that it deals with post-biblical tradition inadequately. There are many instances when a succinct paragraph of church history would have shed far more light than the biblical passages cited. There is, of course, an unbridgeable gap between those Christians who think that the church is Christ in the world, as do Catholics, the Orthodox, and some Protestants, and those who do not. Paradoxically, though, the latter "Bible Christians" espouse many beliefs that only post-biblical tradition delivered to them in the form they espouse it. Examples of this are the doctrines of the Holy Trinity, of full deity and full humanity in the one person of Jesus Christ, and of Jesus' virginal conception in his mother's womb.

## THE CATECHISM AND THE JEWISH SCRIPTURES

Finally, this volume has to be called supersessionist in its outlook in the way it treats the entire revelation made to the people Israel. It does this in part by stressing the divine authorship of the first Testament much more than the human. The Holy Spirit is, of course, responsible for the whole Bible. All Christians believe this. As the Catechism views things, however, this Spirit of God employed the biblical writers for no other purpose than to prepare for Christ. That God chose this people, loved it, and cherished it for its own sake—"for the sake of the ancestors," as Paul put it (Rom 11:28)—does not come through in these pages. To be sure, in one place (§§ 839–40), the Catechism speaks well of the Jewish people in the words of *Nostra Aetate,* part 4. It also quotes Romans 11:29, where Paul says that the gifts and the call of God to the Jews are irrevocable. Immediately after that, however, Jews are identified as a people that has not accepted Jesus as messiah as "we" have, as if this were the sole distinguishing feature of this people, and as if it were a conscious rejection by all Jews of a gift freely offered.

For the rest, in these pages the guiding Spirit did everything that was done from Abraham's call onward to prepare for Christ. This, in effect, renders the Jews a non-people from 135 onward, the date from which increasingly fewer of them professed faith in him. The Catechism cannot be exculpated by the fact that such was the unanimous conviction of the fathers, just as these men of the years 100–600 were unanimous in their view that their Jewish contemporaries continued to be responsible for Jesus' death on the cross. (See the failure to distinguish among various witnesses to tradition above.) Mercifully, the thorny problem of how "the unanimous consent of the fathers" constitutes authentic tradition in that instance is passed over. But the bland assumption that the biblical history of Israel was but a typology of the antitype who is Christ— and this Catechism affirms it many times—can only mean trouble for Christians no less than for the Jews. It simply is not true. Marcel Dubois, a Dominican on the philosophy faculty of the Hebrew University, recently observed in an interview in the *National Catholic Register* that there was little present hope of eastern or western Christian understanding in Israel of the Israelis because all Christians in that land are supersessionist. They have the conviction that the Israel of the Bible is of the past, that the church substitutes for it fully. Hence they hold all Israelis to be religiously inauthentic and to be dealt with accordingly. The Catechism does not declare this in so many words, but any intelligent reader is likely to deduce it from its pages.


## FURTHER EXAMPLES OF SCRIPTURE IN THE CATECHISM

The many authors of the work under scrutiny would doubtless be puzzled and pained by the present critique. Their work is not only redolent of the Bible; citations from it proliferate on many pages. The texts are given in full with the numbered verses following. If the reference is oblique, the biblical place is indicated discreetly below the line.

Chosen at random is a passage where the heading asks why there is need of a sacrament of reconciliation after baptism. Two numbered paragraphs follow:

§ 1425 "You were washed, you were sanctified, you were justified in the name of the Lord Jesus Christ and in the Spirit of our God" (1 Cor 6:11). The greatness of God's gift to us in the sacraments of Christian initiation must be seen in order to grasp the point at which sin is outlawed for those who have "clothed themselves in Christ" (Gal 3:27). But the apostle John also says: "If we say that we have no sin we deceive ourselves, and the truth is not in us" (1 Jn 1:8). [That statement is doubtfully from the evangelist we call John and the gospel from the apostle, but let it pass.] And the Lord himself taught us to pray: "Forgive us our sins" (Lk 11:4), tying mutual pardon for our sins to the pardon that God grants to our sins.

§ 1426 *Conversion* to Christ, the new birth of baptism, the gift of the Holy Spirit, the body and blood of Christ received as our nourishment, has rendered us "holy and blameless before him" (Eph 1:4), even as the church itself, the spouse of Christ, is "holy and without blemish" before him (Eph 5:27). However, the new life received in Christian initiation has not suppressed the fragility and weakness of human nature, nor the inclination to sin that tradition calls *concupiscence,* which remains in the baptized for them to take issue with in the struggle of Christian life, aided by the grace of Christ. [At that point there is a footnote to Denzinger-Schönmetzer quoting Trent on concupiscence as not being sin, against the reformers.] This struggle is that of conversion with a view to the holiness and the eternal life to which the Lord never ceases to call us. [Again a footnote suggesting another Tridentine reference and a place in *Lumen Gentium.*]

The use of the Bible here cannot be faulted in any particular. One might only have wished for references to the concupiscence that is the pull toward sin but not sin itself that are to be found in the Bible, such as Genesis 4:7.

Now for another, less felicitous example of the citation of holy writ, of which there are many. Under the heading "The Immaculate Conception" (§ 490), after perfectly apposite citations

of Luke 1:28 ("most highly favored one," here rendered traditionally "full of grace"), the carefully worded decree of Pius IX in
1854, and its echo in *Lumen Gentium,* 56, we read: "More than any
other created person, the Father has 'blessed her with every spiritual blessing in the heavenly places, in Christ'" (Eph 1:3).

By a device that the French language is capable of and English is not, the pronoun "her" precedes the quotation marks. Ephesians, of course, has said "us," all the baptized, and although Mary
is pre-eminent among us creatures on other grounds, Ephesians
has nothing to say on the subject. In the next sentence, by dint of
the same grammatical device, "[The Father] has chosen *her* in him
[Christ] before the foundation of the world to be holy and blameless before him in love." But the words "holy and blameless" are
applied to Mary by the church in a quite different way than to all
the baptized.

Mark well that the divine liturgy often employs Bible texts in
an accommodated sense such as this. So do the fathers and doctors of the church. It is by way of no harm for a modern book to
do so, provided in our post-enlightenment age it makes clear what
is going on. The *Catechism of the Catholic Church* never does this,
never tells you the rules of interpretation it is operating under.
*Dommage!* Or should one say, in light of the language that prevails
where this volume claims its pedigree, *Peccato!*

# DOES THE CATECHISM REFLECT A HIERARCHY OF TRUTHS?

# Berard L. Marthaler

In 1989 a provisional draft of what is now the *Catechism of the Catholic Church* was sent to the bishops of the world for their criticisms and suggestions. One of the main concerns expressed by American critics was that the Catechism did not respect the principle of hierarchy of truths that the *General Catechetical Directory* said catechesis should take into account "on all levels" (§ 43).

According to Bishop Christoph Schönborn, this American criticism caused the Catechism commission appointed by Pope John Paul II to be "particularly concerned about this issue of the hierarchy of truths."[1] Cardinal Joseph Ratzinger, president of the commission, speaking to the Synod of Bishops in 1990, referred to it as "a recurring criticism," adding, "it is not always easy to know what everyone means by this formula and even less to find clear guidelines as to the manner of accomplishing it." At the time of his report to the synod, Cardinal Ratzinger anticipated that the Preface to the Catechism would explain "the term in light of Vatican Council II and by the *General Catechetical Directory*."[2] The *GCD*, itself based on the Decree on Ecumenism (*Unitatis Redintegratio*) of Vatican II, explains:

> In the message of salvation there is a certain hierarchy of truths, which the church has always recognized when it composed creeds or summaries of the truths of faith. This hierarchy does not mean that some truths pertain to faith itself less than others, but rather that some truths are based on others as of a higher priority, and are illumined by them (n. 11).

> On all levels catechesis should take account of this hierarchy of the truths of faith (n. 43).

Although the explanation that Cardinal Ratzinger anticipated does not appear in the final text of the *Catechism of the Catholic Church,* the Catechism makes two explicit references to the hierarchy of the truths of faith. In my mind, it is the second, § 234, that provides the key to reading and interpreting the new Catechism:

> The central mystery of Christian faith and life is the Trinity, because it is a mystery of God in himself and so the source of all other mysteries of faith, the light that enlightens them, and the most fundamental and essential dogma in the "hierarchy of the truths of the faith." The history of salvation is identical with the history of the way and plan by which the one true God, the Father, Son and Holy Spirit, reveals himself "and reconciles and unites himself with those who turn away from sin."

The orientation of all four parts of the *Catechism of the Catholic Church* is to relate Christian doctrine to the Holy Trinity. Book One, taking the baptismal creed as its point of departure, explains the threefold movement of the divine economy: the work of creation attributed to the Father, redemption to his Son, Jesus Christ, and the ongoing task of sanctification to the Holy Spirit. Later I shall describe the summary statements that round off each unit of the Catechism, but here let me quote four that provide the foundation for all the other books.

> The Most Holy Trinity is the central mystery of Christian faith and life. God alone can make it known by self-revelation as Father, Son and Holy Spirit (§ 261).

> The incarnation of God's Son reveals that God is the eternal Father, the Son is of one being with the Father and Christ is one and the same God in and with the Father (§ 262).

> The mission of the Holy Spirit, sent by the Father in the name of the Son (Jn 14:26) and by the Son "from the Father" (Jn 15:26), reveals that he is, in and with them, one and the same God. "With the Father and the Son he is worshiped and glorified" (§ 263).

By the grace of baptism "in the name of the Father and of the Son and of the Holy Spirit," we are called to share in the life of the Blessed Trinity, already here on earth, "in the obscurity of faith and after death in eternal light" (cf. Paul VI, *Credo of the People of God,* n. 9) (§ 265).

Book Two, "The Celebration of the Christian Mystery," describes "the communication or dispensation of the fruits of Christ's paschal mystery through the celebration of the sacramental liturgy" (§ 1076). It explains how the entirety of the church's liturgical life, the signs and seasons, the sacraments and sacramentals, has the Holy Trinity both as its source and its goal: God's plan of salvation, "accomplished once for all through Christ Jesus in the Holy Spirit, is made present in the sacred actions of the Church's liturgy" (§ 15).

Book Two draws heavily on Vatican II's Constitution on the Sacred Liturgy (*Sacrosanctum Concilium*) and the General Instruction on the Roman Missal. The influence of the eastern tradition is particularly evident in the prominence that the Catechism assigns to the Holy Spirit and on the *epiclesis*—the invocation of the Spirit— in each sacrament.

[Sacraments] are efficacious because Christ himself is at work in them. It is he who baptizes; it is he who acts in all his sacraments in order to communicate the grace that each sacrament signifies. The Father always hears the prayer of his Son's church, which, in the epiclesis of each sacrament, expresses its faith in the Spirit's power. As fire transforms into itself everything it touches, so the Holy Spirit transforms into the divine life whatever is subjected to his power (§ 1127).

The *Catechism of the Catholic Church* says that catechesis has an intrinsic link to "the whole of liturgical and sacramental activity, for it is in the sacraments, especially in the eucharist, that Christ Jesus acts in all his fullness for the transformation of human beings" (§ 1074). The introductory paragraphs that give the reasons for ordering the sacraments under the headings of sacraments of Christian initiation, sacraments of healing, and sacraments at the service of communion and mission (classifications that have long been incorporated by U.S. publishers into catechetical materials) acknowledge that, while this is not the only possible order, it "allows us to view the sacraments as an organic whole in which each has its own vital place." Further, it assigns the eucharist, "the sacrament of sacraments," a unique place in this whole. Quoting St. Thomas, it says "all the other sacraments are ordered to it as their end" (§ 1211). In other passages the Catechism reminds the faithful of the social dimensions of the eucharist, stating that it "directs our concern toward the poor," and "impels Christians to unity" (§§ 1397, 1398).

Although the Trinitarian motif is less explicit in Book Three, "Life in Christ," it is clearly implied, especially in Part One, which describes the human vocation as "Life in the Spirit." It takes as a fundamental principle that "the creation of the human person in the image and likeness of God is the basis for human dignity which is fulfilled in the vocation to divine happiness" (§ 1700). Quoting St. Paul, the Catechism attributes to the Holy Spirit the power to live the Christian life:

> "Justified in the name of the Lord Jesus Christ and the Spirit of our God" and "sanctified in Christ Jesus and called to be saints," Christians have become temples of the *Holy Spirit*. This Spirit of the Son, who has become the source of our life, teaches us to pray to the Father, crying out "Abba!" The Spirit guides our actions, that we might bear his fruit by love in action. The Spirit heals the wounds of sin, renews us inwardly by a spiritual transformation, and enlightens and strengthens us to live as children of light, in all that is good and right and true (§ 1695).

The theme of Book Four is "Christian Prayer." The Catechism describes prayer as "a covenant relationship in Christ between the believer and God" (§ 2564), and in another place as "encounter between God and humanity" (§ 2626). It distinguishes five forms of Christian prayer—blessing, adoration, petition, intercession, thanksgiving and praise—and finds the Holy Trinity active in each form. For example, the Catechism identifies two fundamental movements in the prayer of blessing:

> . . . our prayer *ascends* in the Holy Spirit through Christ to the Father—we bless him for having blessed us; it implores the grace of the Holy Spirit that *descends* through Christ from the Father— he blesses us (§ 2627).

The last section of the Catechism is a meditative explanation of the Lord's Prayer. Quoting Tertullian, it says that the Lord's Prayer "is truly the summary of the whole gospel" (§ 2761), and warns that it is not a formula to be repeated "mechanically."

> As in every vocal prayer, it is by God's word that the Holy Spirit teaches God's children to speak to their Father. Jesus gives not only the words of our filial prayer, he gives us at the same time the Spirit by whom these words become in us "spirit and life." . . . Prayer to our Father is assumed into the mysterious mission of his Son and Spirit (§ 2766).

## THE UNFOLDING OF THE MYSTERY

As the central mystery of Christian faith and life (§ 232), the Holy Trinity is the source from which all other truths of faith flow and have their meaning. The 2,865 paragraphs of the *Catechism of the Catholic Church* all relate in some way to that mystery. Passages that describe the nature and means of revelation whereby the mystery of the triune God has been made known are the very foundation of Christianity. The first article of the Creed, "I/We believe," is the most fundamental. All the other articles depend on it, and it "helps us to know God better as he is revealed progressively to us" (§ 199).

The revelation of the Holy Trinity enjoys highest priority in the hierarchy of truths, especially when it relates to the person and mission of Christ Jesus. Just as the Catechism presents Trinitarian theology and christology as two facets of the same mystery, so must catechesis emphasize their mutual relationship.

> At the heart of catechesis is a person, Jesus of Nazareth, the Father's only Son, who suffered and died for us and, after rising from the dead, now lives with us forever. To catechize is to set forth, in Christ's person, the fullness of God's eternal plan and to seek understanding of the meaning of Christ's actions, words and signs. Catechesis aims at putting people not only in touch but in intimate communion with Jesus Christ, who alone can lead us in the Spirit to the Father's love and enable us to share in the life of the Holy Trinity (§ 426).

The Catechism makes it clear that in the hierarchy of truths "the articles of faith concerning his incarnation and passover illuminate his [Jesus'] whole earthly life" (§ 512). Everything he did, "from the beginning until the day when he was taken up to heaven, is seen in the light of the mysteries of Christmas and Easter" (§ 512). It is important to note in this text and elsewhere that the Catechism consistently uses the term "mysteries" in speaking of Jesus' earthly life. The Catechism refers not to *events* but to *mysteries* of his hidden and public life. Catechesis is concerned with sharing the life of Christ and not with speculation that only feeds human curiosity.

The paschal mystery that sums up the mission of Christ Jesus in the world achieves fulfillment in the outpouring of the Holy Spirit. The article in the Creed concerning the church "depends entirely on the article about the Holy Spirit, which immediately precedes it" (§ 749). The Catechism, quoting *Ad gentes* of Vatican II, presents the church's missionary mandate as grounded in the missions of the Son and Spirit. It adds, "The church's supreme mission is to enable people to share in the communion between the Father and the Son in their Spirit of love" (§ 850).

In another place, the Catechism makes it clear that

> the church's mission is not an addition to that of Christ and the Holy Spirit, but is its sacrament: in its whole being and in all its members, the church is sent to proclaim, bear witness, make present and spread the mystery of the communion of the Holy Trinity . . . (§ 738).

## ORGANIC UNITY OF THE TRUTHS OF FAITH

Earlier I noted that the *Catechism of the Catholic Church* makes two explicit references to the hierarchy of truths. Up to this point I have elaborated on the reference that links the hierarchy of truths to the mystery of the Trinity and the economy of salvation. Now I turn to the other reference, which links the hierarchy of truths to the "mutual connections and coherence of dogmas . . . found in the context of the whole revelation of the Christian mystery" (§ 90). While seeking to avoid the impression that all its declarations are of equal importance, the authors of the Catechism emphasize the organic unity of the truths of faith. "A vital connection" exists between dogmas—truths proposed by the teaching authority of the church—and the spiritual life.

> . . . dogmas are beacons along the path of faith; they illumine it and make it safe. Conversely, if our lives are going in the right direction, our intellects and hearts will be open to accept the light shed by dogmas of faith (§ 89).

In outlining criteria for the interpretation of scripture the *Catechism of the Catholic Church* introduces the notion of *analogy of faith*. Defined as "the coherence of the truths of faith among themselves and in the context of the entire plan of salvation" (§ 114), "analogy of faith" is an important norm for interpreting the Catechism itself.

In his report to the 1990 Synod of Bishops Cardinal Ratzinger stressed that the principle of hierarchy of truths implies the "organic unity, the 'symphony' of truth, the central reference of which is Jesus Christ."[3] The same point was made in the *Dossier Informativo* published by the Editorial Commission of the Catechism of the Catholic Church.[4] While respecting the distinction between divinely revealed truths and other truths proposed by the church, the Catechism intends to establish the relationship of the mysteries of faith to one another—*nexus mysteriorum*—and their reference to the center, which is Christ. Both Cardinal Ratzinger and the *Dossier Informativo* assert that the four-part structure of the Catechism establishes the relationship between the *lex credendi, lex orandi,* and *lex vivendi.*

The hierarchy of truths is not, as Cardinal Ratzinger has noted, the same as degree of certainty. He belonged (as I do) to a generation of theologians who, in addition to studying the church's teaching, had to learn whether a particular thesis (statement) was something revealed and, if revealed, whether the church had solemnly affirmed it either by conciliar definition or by papal declaration. And then there were teachings of the ordinary magisterium, commonly held but never defined, as well as speculative opinions of theologians. Each thesis carried an annotation (*nota theologica*) that in effect assigned a greater or lesser degree of certainty to it.

The approach was criticized and ultimately repudiated by contemporary theologians for a number of reasons. Instead of appearing as an elucidation of the gospel message, church doctrine appeared as a series of teachings whose relationship to each other was not always clear. Some teachings were obviously basic, but there was a tendency to regard teachings that did not merit the annotation "revealed" or "defined" (as, for example, the church's social teachings) to be of secondary importance and marginal to the essential message. The *Catechism of the Catholic Church* emphasizes the organic unity of Christian doctrine.

To insure that each theme is seen as part of the whole, the Catechism uses a number of bibliographic devices. Each of the four books begins with an introduction that summarizes its main themes and links them to the other books. Numerous cross-references in the margins, as well as an analytical index at the end of the volume, refer the reader to other passages where the topic is touched on. The Catechism's effort to establish the interrelation of the truths of faith to each other and to the whole has led to a certain amount of unavoidable repetition.

On the other hand, to avoid the misconception that everything it states is of equal importance, the Catechism identifies certain passages of "secondary historical, apologetic or doctrinal importance" by the use of small print (§ 20). A few examples illustrate their wide diversity:

*Historical.* The Catechism (in large print) assigns to the gospels "the supreme place" among the books of the Bible. Then, citing *Dei Verbum* of Vatican II, it states, "We can distinguish three stages in the formation of the gospels," that it identifies in small print as the life and teaching of Jesus, the oral tradition, and, finally, the written gospels themselves (§ 126).

*Apologetic.* In explaining that in Christ we have the fullness of revelation that will never pass away, the Catechism expresses a word of caution about revelations that claim to supplement if not supplant it.

> The Christian faith cannot accept "revelations" that pretend to surpass or correct the revelation of which Christ is the fulfillment, as is the case in certain non-Christian religions and also in certain recent sects which based themselves on such new "revelations" yet still claim to be Christian (§ 67).

*Doctrinal.* In stressing the importance of catechesis on the meaning and purpose of creation the Catechism identifies two questions as "decisive": one question is about the origins, the other about the purpose (§ 282). In small print it goes on to explain,

> The question of the origins of the world and of the human race has been the object of many scientific studies which have greatly enriched our knowledge of the age and dimensions of the cosmos, the development of life forms and the appearance of humanity. These discoveries summon forth even greater admiration for the creator, prompting us to give him thanks for all his works and for the understanding and wisdom he gives to researchers and the learned . . . (§ 283).

Each of the foregoing examples, three among many, illustrates how the *Catechism of the Catholic Church* first sets out the main point of the church's teaching and then expands on specific points. Some are biblical quotations; some cite conciliar teachings; some make reference, however oblique, to contemporary questions. Every quotation must be considered on its own merits because not all are of equal authority, and those that deal with the finer points of doctrine (e.g. the *filioque*, §§ 247–248) are generally beyond the ordinary believer. Common sense and pastoral concerns must dictate their use in catechetical instruction. The fact that these teachings are set in small type, however, does not suggest that the church is uncertain about their place in the overall hierarchy of truths of the faith and their value in expounding the profundity of the Christian message.

Other passages in small type, quotations from patristic, liturgical, magisterial, or hagiographical sources, "have often been chosen with a view to their direct catechetical use." They too are specifically "intended to enrich the doctrinal presentations" (§ 21) but, even more, their purpose is to witness to the church's faith, its catholicity and continuity. It is not surprising that the Catechism draws on the church fathers, liturgical texts, and papal statements of all kinds, but one is struck by the number of quotations from autobiographies and biographies of saints. On the one hand, they clearly represent a conscious effort to stress the importance of Christian witness, and, on the other hand, they indicate the importance of the lives of the saints in catechesis.

And then there is a series of short texts in small italic type. These are the "In Brief" statements that have attracted an undue amount of attention. The Catechism describes them as summing up "the essentials of that unit's teaching in condensed formulas that may suggest to local catechists brief summaries that can be memorized" (§ 22). In all there are some 550 "In Brief" texts drawn from the scriptures, liturgy, writings of the church fathers and theologians, magisterial statements, including the documents of Vatican II, and the Code of Canon Law. Commenting on these texts in an address to the International Catechetical Commission in September 1992, Cardinal Ratzinger explained their purpose at some length. He described them as "synthetic propositions that sum up in simple and essential form important themes." They articulate the essence of the church's faith and provide insights into the fundamental character of Christian identity as it has come to be better refined over the ages. The cardinal said that these "In Brief" statements serve as models to today's Christians who, drawing on the inexhaustible source of the church's tradition, must express the faith in a concrete way and in meaningful language.[5]

According to Cardinal Ratzinger, these summary statements, properly adapted to the learners, will contribute to an affective and intellectual appreciation of the faith based on understanding and memory. In addition to providing "conceptual and terminological precision," they "promote the acquisition of a common language of faith" respectful of heritage and witnessing to the Catholic dimension of the Christian faith that transcends culture. It must be stressed, moreover, that the "In Brief" texts do not have a life of their own. They are closely linked to the paragraphs that precede them and that provide the context for a correct understanding of their meaning.

## HIERARCHY AMONG THE CREEDS AND WITHIN THE CREED

The use of small type is the most obvious means that the *Catechism of the Catholic Church* uses to avoid giving the impression that everything it teaches is of equal importance. But the Catechism calls attention to the hierarchy of truths in other ways. We have already mentioned that there is a hierarchy of importance in the parts of the Catechism itself. All four books form a whole and should be read together, but the explanation of the Creed in Book One is the foundation on which the others rest. Like most Christians, Catholics assign a normative value to the ancient creeds. The Trinitarian faith professed in the baptismal creed is the heart of the liturgy, the *raison d'être* of the Christian life and the inspiration for prayer.

The Catechism acknowledges that circumstances have forced the church to articulate its faith in different ways through the centuries. By way of illustration it cites, among others, the *Quicumque* (also called the Athanasian Creed), professions of faith of various councils (including that of Trent), and Pope Paul VI's *Credo of the People of God* (§ 192). These summaries "help us today to attain and deepen the enduring faith," but not all enjoy equal authority. Notwithstanding that none "can be considered superseded or irrelevant," the Catechism makes it clear that the Apostles' Creed and the Nicene Creed "occupy a special place in the church's life," the former because of its antiquity, the latter because "it stems from the first two ecumenical councils" and "remains common to all the great churches of both east and west to this day" (§§ 193–196). The Catechism quotes other creeds, but it takes its basic outline from these ancient professions of faith.

We have already noted the hierarchy of truths within the creed itself, but this extends also to the commandments:

> "I believe in God": this first affirmation of the Apostles' Creed is also the most fundamental. The entire Creed speaks of God, and when it also speaks of humanity and of the world, it does so in relation to God. The other articles of the Creed all depend on the first, even as the remaining nine commandments make the first explicit: "You shall love the Lord your God with all your heart, and with all your soul, and with all your might." The other articles help us to know God better as he is revealed progressively to us . . . (§ 199).

Catechetical tradition, following Jesus himself, has always singled out the twofold commandment—love of God and love of neighbor—as the basis of Christian ethics. The *Catechism of the Catholic Church* reaffirms this in stating, "The decalogue must be interpreted in light of this twofold yet single commandment of love, the fulfillment of the law" (§ 2055).

The bishops responsible for drafting the *Catechism of the Catholic Church* were very careful to emphasize the basic, essential, and immutable message of Christianity, and to distinguish it from the way that message has been expressed and elaborated in various times and circumstances. Cardinal Ratzinger reports that the drafters also tried "as much as possible to avoid theological opinions, both by not preferring one or the other particular theological synthesis and by not closing particular questions that remain open and that are the object of theological research and reflection."[6]

## INTERPRETING THE CATECHISM

The *Catechism of the Catholic Church* recognizes that the church proposes doctrine at several levels of authority (§§ 891, 892). The committee originally charged with rendering the Catechism into English tried to assist the reader in sorting these different levels out by its use of language. When it is a matter of a doctrine that the church has solemnly defined, they used one of the following phrases: "confesses/professes; solemnly/definitively teaches." When doctrines are not solemnly defined but are taught by the ordinary magisterium, the translators said that the church "teaches." When it is a matter of the overall content of Catholic teaching, referred to in a global but not technically precise way, the English text had that the church "commonly teaches/holds." The English translation, at least initially, tried to make these distinctions clearly and consistently.

In his article in this collection on the authority of the Catechism, my colleague Joseph Komonchak notes that in explaining particular teachings of the Catechism

> the classical norms of theological interpretations will have to be invoked: the character and authority of the sources from which the doctrines are drawn, the frequency and universality with which they are taught, the style of the texts in which they are proposed, etc. Inclusion of various elements in the new Catechism will not by itself settle the issue of the varying degrees of authority that lie behind them.[7]

Komonchak finds support for this position in the words of Bishop Schönborn, who writes, "The level of certainty of the doctrines must be . . . derived from the context, from the modes of expression, from the doctrinal authority of the affirmation."[8] The bishops, for whom the work is primarily intended, will appreciate these distinctions. Publishers, priests, catechists and other faithful who read the *Catechism of the Catholic Church* will need to look to the guidance of specialists who are familiar with the Catholic theological tradition and terminology. There is something for everyone in these pages that witness, inform, and inspire. The Catechism was studiously planned and carefully crafted. Readers who would mine its riches cannot approach it with any less care and commitment to study. In the end, we must recognize that the *Catechism of the Catholic Church* is a very sophisticated document, the nuances and subtleties of which will have to be interpreted by experts. And experts, like ordinary readers and the authors of the *Catechism of the Catholic Church* themselves, return to the Apostles' Creed to find the rule of faith that is the framework of the hierarchy of truths of the faith—the Trinitarian doxology.

# WHAT IS OLD AND WHAT IS NEW IN THE CATECHISM?

## Peter C. Phan

In his Apostolic Constitution *Fidei Depositum* presenting the *Catechism of the Catholic Church*,[1] Pope John Paul II compares the Catechism to a scribe who becomes a disciple of the kingdom of heaven and, like a householder, brings out from the storeroom things both new and old (cf. Mt 13:52). The task assigned to me, to determine what is old and what is new in the *CCC*, is indeed a herculean one. It embraces the entire text of more than five hundred pages and requires familiarity with contemporary theology regarding the central articles of faith, worship, morality, and spirituality.

Several preliminary questions beg for clarification before the task of identifying what is old and new in the Catechism can be attempted. For example, what are the works with which the *CCC* should be compared in order to identify its old and new elements? Should not a catechism, by its very nature, refrain from presenting something new? What counts as new, since novelty is a relative term, especially in matters of faith and morals? If there be a novelty, then for whom is it new, since a thing may be old hat to one person and new-fangled innovation to another?

To make my task somewhat manageable, I will compare and contrast the *Catechism of the Catholic Church* with the *Catechismus ex decreto Concilii Tridentini ad Parochos,* published by order of Pope Pius V in 1566, popularly referred to as the *Roman Catechism*,[2] and with the documents of Vatican II. The choice of these texts is not entirely arbitrary. On the one hand, the *CCC*, even though not mandated by the Second Vatican Council, is "composed following the Second Vatican Council," as its subtitle asserts, and therefore is a parallel of the *Roman Catechism* insofar as the latter was commissioned by a general council. On the other hand, the *CCC* is purported to "present an organic synthesis of the foundations and essential content of Catholic doctrine, as regards both faith and morals, *in the light of the Second Vatican Council* and the whole of the Church's tradition" (§ 11, emphasis added). The question then can be raised: How faithful is the *CCC* to the spirit and documents of Vatican II?

It would seem appropriate, therefore, to examine how the *Catechism of the Catholic Church* stands in comparison with the *Roman Catechism* and Vatican II. The comparison and contrast will be carried out in terms of both form and content. Were one to work out the variations on the Lord's saying about new wine and old skins (cf. Mk 2:22; Mt 9:17; Lk 5:37–38), four possibilities emerge: two consistent options, namely, old wine in old skins, and new wine in new skins; and two compromises, namely, new wine in old skins, and old wine in new skins. In terms of form and content, four combinations are possible: old content in old form, new content in new form, new content in old form, and old content in new form. Which of these possibilities does the *CCC* realize?

In the first part of my essay I will point out some of the most salient similarities and differences between the *CCC,* on the one hand, and the *Roman Catechism* and the teaching of Vatican II, on the other. In this way what is old and what is new in the *CCC* in terms of form and structure will be made apparent. In terms of structure, the Catechism is divided into four parts: the Creed, the sacraments, the decalogue, and prayer. To render my remarks on what is substantively old and new in the Catechism more concrete, I will highlight in the second part of the essay what in my judgment constitutes the most conservative and the most innovative features of each of these four sections. In the last part I will make some comments on how these old and new elements of the Catechism should be dealt with in catechesis.

## WHAT IS OLD AND WHAT IS NEW IN THE FORM AND STRUCTURE OF THE *CCC*?

In comparing the *Catechism of the Catholic Church* with the *Roman Catechism,* one common feature stands out at once: both texts are intended primarily for teachers of the faith and pastors of the church, and not directly for the people to be catechized. The *Roman Catechism* is addressed to parish priests, and the *CCC* to bishops and, through them, to priests, catechists, and editors of catechisms, though it is hoped that it will be useful reading for all the faithful. Differently, however, from the *Roman Catechism*, which parish priests were urged to use as a source to expound scripture, the *CCC* is intended to serve "as a point of reference for the catechisms or *compendia* to be composed in various countries" (§ 12). It is not, therefore, a textbook for catechesis.

Secondly, there is in both catechisms a concern, quite explicit in the *Roman Catechism* but no less real in the *CCC*, for an unambiguous and authoritative statement of church teaching in matters of faith and morals. Though the *CCC* goes beyond its predecessor in its emphasis on the need to adapt the presentation of Christian doctrines not only to the individual's age, capacity, and spiritual condition but also to different cultures as well as to ecclesial and social conditions among the people of God, the *CCC* is presented as "a sure and certain standard for the teaching of the faith," and as "a sure and authentic source book for the teaching of Catholic doctrine and especially for the composition of local catechisms."[3]

Thirdly, and more importantly, the *Catechism of the Catholic Church* preserves the four-part division of the *Roman Catechism*. It explicitly admits that its structure is inspired by "great traditional catechisms, which are built on four pillars: the baptismal profession of faith (the Creed), the celebration of faith (the sacraments), the life of faith (the commandments), and the prayers of believers (the Lord's Prayer)" (§ 13).[4] Whether this rigid four-part structure proves to be the old wineskin into which the *CCC* attempts to pour the new wine of Christian doctrine as it has been renewed by Vatican II and by contemporary biblical, historical, systematic, and practical theology is a point that will be examined later.

Beyond these three basic structural similarities between the *Roman Catechism* and the *Catechism of the Catholic Church*, there are three innovations in the new Catechism that deserve mention. The first, minor but rather significant, is the use of Christian art on the cover and at the beginning of each of the four parts of the book. These artistic representations are aptly chosen to introduce the contents of each part.[5] Unfortunately, at least in the French edition, the reproductions are done in black and white rather than in color, and as a consequence some of their beauty has been lost.

Secondly, the *CCC*, in a move that is unusual for a catechism designed for the Latin church, makes abundant use of the writings of the Greek fathers, the canon law of the eastern churches, and especially the eastern liturgies, in particular the liturgy of St. John Chrysostom, the Byzantine liturgy, the Syriac liturgy, and the *Fanqith*. The use of such resources cannot but promote the ecumenical understanding between the Roman and the Orthodox churches.

Thirdly, the *CCC* has introduced a new feature in its composition. At the end of each theme's treatment, it appends a series of brief texts in small italics. These texts are said to sum up "the essentials of that unit's teaching in condensed formulas that may suggest to local catechists brief summaries that can be memorized" (§ 22). Whether these "condensed formulas" are really summaries of the texts that precede them and whether they should and/or can serve the function of "brief summaries to be memorized" are issues to which we shall come back later.

Before proceeding to compare the *Catechism of the Catholic Church* with the documents of Vatican II, it is useful to offer here some reflections on its structure. The *CCC's* adoption of the four-part structure of the *Roman Catechism* has been severely criticized by many commentators as a fundamental flaw. For one thing, it tends to separate faith from liturgical worship, moral praxis, and prayer. The integral unity between faith and life, so strongly affirmed by Vatican II, especially in *Gaudium et Spes*, is sundered. Head, heart, and hand do not act in concert with one another. Despite the claim that the Catechism, "conceived as an organic presentation of the Catholic faith in its entirety, should be read as a whole" (§ 18), and in spite of attempts to link the four parts together by means of cross-references, the Catechism fails to unfold the organic unity between Christian faith and orthopraxis. This monumental failure must be attributed to the *CCC's* desire to keep the old things of the catechetical storeroom, to preserve the old wineskins for the new wine.

Furthermore, just as the old skins would burst if the new wine were poured into them, and the wine would spill, and both the skins and the wine be lost, so the four-part scheme proves to be the procrustean bed upon which a host of new theological issues are forced to lie. As a result, both the scheme and the doctrines suffer. This is especially true in the sections on the Creed and the decalogue. One example from each section will suffice.

The christological treatment (§§ 422–682) is severely handicapped by the limitations of the six creedal formulas regarding Jesus. The approach of the Creed is a descending christology, which emphasizes the divinity of Jesus. The Catechism, constrained by this approach, tends to downplay Jesus' humanity, which contemporary ascending christology strongly emphasizes. Moreover, because the Creed says nothing about Jesus' life before his crucifixion, the *CCC* is forced to devote a separate section on "the mysteries of the life of Christ" (§§ 512–570), which is, however, not well integrated into its christology. Similarly, because one of the creedal formulas about Christ confesses that Jesus was "born of the Virgin Mary," the Catechism treats of Mary's predestination, immaculate conception, divine motherhood, and virginity in its christological section (§§ 487–511). Later, in the section on the church, the Catechism returns to mariology, presumably because *Lumen Gentium* locates Mary in the church, even though the ninth article of the Creed, which confesses faith in the one Catholic Church and the communion of saints, does not mention Mary.

Artificial and cramped distribution of material is also evident in the section on the decalogue. Formulated in an entirely different set of circumstances, the decalogue is pressed to serve as a framework for a discussion of the moral issues of our times, a function it obviously cannot fulfill. What the third part of the Catechism offers, then, is neither a standard exegesis of the literal meaning of Exodus 20:1–17 nor a theological elaboration of such a meaning. Rather it uses the decalogue as an occasion or excuse to state the official teaching on moral issues, many of which the decalogue could not even envisage. For instance, the much-admired social teaching of the church is maneuvered to fit into the fourth, fifth, sixth, seventh, ninth, and tenth commandments. Here as well as in the section on the Creed, the *CCC* can hardly be exculpated from the charges of artificiality, disjointedness, and disorganization.

A word or two about the "condensed formulas" is also in order. Rhetorically, it is highly questionable that the most effective way to summarize a densely discursive and theologically charged text is by means of a series of unconnected, at times cryptic, statements. Moreover, the fact that these formulas are presented as suggesting to local catechists "brief summaries to be memorized" (§ 22) reinforces the idea that catechesis is ultimately a matter of teaching orthodox formulas to be learned by heart. Indeed, given the extraordinarily large number of these sometimes lengthy summaries, only those blessed with amazingly retentive powers can be expected to commit them to memory. There is also the great danger that these formulas will be detached from their contexts and used as free-floating mantras. It goes without saying that such a use is exceedingly misleading. For instance, to affirm *tout court* that "the old law is a preparation for the gospel" (§ 1982) runs the risk of anti-semitism. Worse, these formulas can be turned into shibboleths by conservatives to gauge the orthodoxy of current or future catechisms.

With regard to Vatican II, it is obvious that the *Catechism of the Catholic Church* depends extensively upon the conciliar texts. All sixteen conciliar documents are cited, with those on the liturgy, the church, revelation, and the church in the modern world taking the lion's share of attention. In this respect, the *CCC* does contain new elements in comparison with its predecessor. There is, however, irony here. Whereas the four-part structure of the *Roman Catechism* represents the old skins into which the new wine is poured, the documents of Vatican II may be said to be the new skins into which the old wine is carefully decanted. Indeed, while Vatican II is copiously cited, its spirit, as many commentators have lamented, is conspicuously absent.

Two examples will illustrate this point. First, with regard to ecclesiology: Though the final text of the *CCC* is a vast improvement over the provisional text, what Avery Dulles said about the ecclesiology contained in the provisional text still largely applies:

> The fidelity to Vatican II, moreover, is incomplete. Certain teachings of the council are indeed repeated, but many of its concerns, such as *aggiornamento*, the reformability of the church, the importance of the word of God, the structure of collegiality, the active role of the laity, the value of the religious life, regional diversification, and ecumenism, are skirted or suppressed. A stronger case for evangelization and for the social mission of the church would be desirable.[6]

While some of Dulles' criticisms have been met in the final version of the *CCC*, which notes the value of the religious life (§§ 914–933) and, to a lesser extent, regional diversification (§ 887), there is still lacking a distinctive "communion ecclesiology" that is the hallmark of Vatican II.[7] There is a heavy emphasis on the hierarchical structure of the church and on the laity's duty of obedience to the magisterium, especially in moral matters.

The second example concerns the Catechism's teaching on the sacraments (§§ 1210–1666). Though quoting Vatican II abundantly in this section, it chooses to structure the sacramental system through the analogy with the development of human life, especially physical life, that is proposed by Thomas Aquinas.[8] This means that, as David Power has pointed out, the *CCC* has favored the post-Tridentine approach to the sacraments with its emphasis on institution, essential rite, qualities of minister and recipient, and sacramental effects.[9]

To return to our question about what is old and what is new in the form and structure of the *Catechism of the Catholic Church*, the answer is that with reference to both the *Roman Catechism* and Vatican II, the *CCC*'s form and structure is both new and old. In particular, the four-part structure is the old skin into which the new wine is poured, and Vatican II is the new skin into which the old wine is decanted. This is, in my judgment, the fundamental cause of the tension and even inconsistency that critics perceive in the *CCC*.

## WHAT IS OLD AND WHAT IS NEW IN THE CONTENTS OF THE *CCC*?

It is of course impossible to list all the old and new elements in the teachings of the Catechism; my intention here is to highlight, somewhat arbitrarily, those doctrines contained in the four parts of the *CCC* that may be of interest to catechists and those who are professionally concerned with the teaching of the faith.

I. *The Profession of Faith.* One naturally does not expect much doctrinal innovation from a catechism; after all, it is not a theological treatise proffering the latest hypotheses or seeking to be on the cutting edge of research. There is much, then, especially in the exposition of the Creed, that is traditional, and therefore "old."

There are, however, elements in the *CCC's* exposition of the Creed that are "old" in the pejorative sense of outmoded. For example, in its interpretation of the formula "he descended to the dead,"[10] the Catechism seems to take it literally to mean that Jesus descended into the realm of the dead (§§ 632–633). It states rather baldly in the subsequent condensed formula (which is to be memorized!) that "in his human soul joined to his divine person, the dead Christ descended to the dead and opened the gates of heaven for the just who had preceded him in death" (§ 637). While such an interpretation is not to be ruled out of court, it would have helped matters immeasurably to state unambiguously that such a phrase need not be taken literally and that other interpretations (such as Hans Urs von Balthasar's or Karl Rahner's) are theologically plausible. The same thing should be said of the *CCC*'s interpretation of the last things, especially of the fire of purgatory (§ 1031).

On the other hand, there are (relatively) novel insights that deserve special mention. For the first time in a universal catechism there is recognized the necessity of distinguishing the apostolic tradition from "the various theological, disciplinary, liturgical or devotional traditions, born in the local churches over time, which are the particular forms in which tradition receives expressions adapted to different places and times" (§ 83). Though these lines are printed in small letters in the text, they are of immense importance for catechesis insofar as a sound catechetical pedagogy requires one to take into account the hierarchy of truths. Indeed, would that the *CCC* itself had followed its own counsel and distinguished more clearly in its exposition what is of faith and what is a particular theological tradition!

Another theologically significant feature of the Catechism with respect to older catechisms is its pneumatology (§§ 683–747). As Francis J. Buckley has commented, this section is "a model of what the Catechism could be: warm, even poetic, with a fine eye for patterns that pull the material together and intensify the response of faith."[11] It presents in a well-ordered and integrated fashion the unity of the missions of Jesus and the Spirit, the various names and symbols of the Spirit, the working of the Spirit in the history of Israel, of Jesus, and of the church.

II. *The Celebration of the Christian Mystery.* I have already mentioned the unfortunate decision of the Catechism to structure the sacramental system according to the model of human growth. One of the consequences of this model is the division of the sacraments into three groups: the sacraments of initiation, corresponding to birth and growth (baptism, confirmation, and eucharist), the sacraments of healing (penance and anointing), and the sacraments at the service of the faithful's communion and mission (orders and marriage).

Three negative effects of this odd classification result for sacramental theology. First, the centrality of the eucharist as the "source and summit of the whole Christian life" (*Lumen Gentium,* no. 11) is obscured; its integrating and unifying function for all liturgical and sacramental celebrations is lost. Secondly, while it is legitimate to view orders and marriage as contributing to the communion among the faithful, the sacrament of communion *par excellence* is the eucharist; to speak of the communion of the church apart from the eucharist is a serious flaw. Thirdly, in this model the celebration of the sacraments is primarily an affair of the individual, geared toward his or her spiritual growth; the sacraments are detached from the matrix of the history of salvation and from their ecclesial context. In short, an institutional and instrumental theology of the sacraments still prevails in the *CCC*.

Besides this antiquated division of the sacramental system, there is also in the Catechism a neo-scholastic approach to the theology of the sacraments themselves. Mention has already been made of its focus on such institutional and juridical issues as institution, essential rites, minister and recipient, and effects of the sacraments. Both the systematization and the theology of the sacraments in the *CCC* are carry-overs of the old sacramental theology.

In comparison with the *Roman Catechism* and other older catechetical texts, the *Catechism of the Catholic Church* has made at least three notable advances in its treatment of the sacraments and liturgical worship. First, it offers a profound explanation of how the liturgy and sacramental celebrations are the work of the Trinity (§§ 1077–1112). In them "the Father is blessed and worshiped as the source of all the blessing of creation and salvation" (§ 1110); "the Son's work in the liturgy is sacramental" (§ 1111); "the mission of the Holy Spirit in the church's liturgy is to prepare the assembly to encounter Christ, to recall and reveal Christ to the believing assembly, to make Christ's saving work present and actual in the church by his transforming power and to make this gift of communion bear fruit" (§ 1112).

Secondly, the Catechism recognizes the importance of popular devotions and religiosity for developing an authentic Christian life and urges that they be fostered and corrected whenever necessary. It quotes an extensive passage from the document of Puebla which affirms that "at its core the religiosity of the people is a storehouse of values that offers the answers of Christian wisdom to the great questions of life" (§ 1676).

Thirdly, for the first time, a universal catechism recognizes that liturgical diversity and ritual pluralism is a source of enrichment for the church:

> Christ's mystery is so boundlessly rich that no single liturgical tradition can exhaust its expression. The history of the appearance and development of the various rites demonstrates their remarkable complementarity. When particular churches observe their respective liturgical traditions in communion of faith and sacraments, they enrich one another and grow in fidelity to the whole church's tradition and common mission (§ 1201).

In addition, the *CCC* urges that the celebration of the liturgy correspond to the genius and culture of different peoples. It hastens to add that there are immutable elements as well as elements subject to change in the liturgy and the sacraments, and that only the latter can and must be adapted to the various cultures. It cautions that diversity must not damage unity and that the new forms must remain faithful to the common faith, to the sacramental signs given by Christ, and to hierarchical communion. Finally, it notes that "cultural adaptation also requires a conversion of heart and even, where necessary, a breaking with ancestral customs incompatible with the Catholic faith" (§ 1206).

In my judgment, the Catechism's understanding of cultural adaptation still remains at the superficial level of cross-cultural "translation" by dynamic equivalence and falls short of genuine inculturation understood as liberation, transformation, and synthesis of culture.[12] Nevertheless, the acknowledgement of the enrichment of the church by liturgical diversity and of the necessity of liturgical inculturation is an important step in the process of making Christian worship a genuinely catholic celebration.

III. *Life in Christ.* Perhaps less innovation is to be expected of the *CCC* in the area of morals than in that of faith. After all, the Roman magisterium is known for its conservatism in moral matters, especially regarding sexuality. I have already pointed out that the Catechism's use of the ancient decalogue as a framework for expounding Christian morality proves to be the straitjacket hampering a systematic elaboration of a well-ordered moral theology.

It must be admitted that the definitive text of the *CCC* is a vast improvement over the provisional text, whose legalistic approach is overwhelming. Nevertheless, there are at least two aspects in which the *CCC* resembles an old neo-scholastic moral treatise. First, its approach to morality is act-centered rather than focused on the agent. There is no discussion of the agent's fundamental option or stance in determining the morality of his or her act. Rather the goodness or badness of an act is determined by "the *object* chosen, the *intention* or end foreseen, the *circumstances* of the action" (§ 1750). This view is particularly evident in the Catechism's teaching on mortal and venial sins. Mortal sin, it says in quoting John Paul II's *Reconciliatio et poenitentia* (n. 17), "is sin whose object is grave matter and which is committed with full knowledge and deliberate consent" (§ 1857). Similarly, there is an objectivist and legalistic note in its definition of venial sin: "We commit *venial* sins when we do not observe the moderation prescribed by the moral law in less serious matters, or when we disobey the moral law in grave matters, but without full knowledge or complete consent" (§ 1862).

Another area in which the *CCC* reflects the old moral theology is its understanding of natural law. It is well known that Roman Catholic ethics is committed to an objective moral order and this commitment is expressed in its acceptance of the concept of natural law. However, in recent decades, there has been a strong affirmation of historical consciousness; to use Bernard Lonergan's terms, there has been a change from the classicist to the empirical understanding of culture. The classicist culture views natural law as a universal and permanent human product normative for all peoples and all times. The modern, empirical notion of culture regards natural law as a nexus of meanings constituted by free and responsible incarnated subjects, differing from peoples to peoples, and capable of development and decay.[13] This cultural shift effectively undermines the claim of a particular nexus of myths and symbols and a particular set of rules to universal normativity.

The *CCC* rightly emphasizes the objectivity of natural law, but it appears to be too sanguine about the possibility of formulating concrete moral norms that would be valid in all situations. It tends to favor a deductive method over a more experiential and inductive one and belittles the relevance of culture and history in the formulation and reformulation of specific moral norms. For instance, while recognizing that "applications of the natural law vary greatly and after due reflection should be adapted to the diversity of life's conditions, according to places, times, and circumstances" (§ 1957), the Catechism states that "[t]he natural law is unchangeable and permanent throughout the variations of history. It is present under the flux of ideas and customs and sustains their progress. The rules that express it remain substantially valid" (§ 1958). It seems that for the *CCC* the formulations of the natural law are done apart from culture and history and that it is only in their applications that variety and diversity occur.

Furthermore, recent Catholic moral theology has attempted to integrate the natural law approach to morality with the biblical approach that emphasizes story-telling and views Christian life as discipleship to Jesus. The *CCC* discusses the natural law, the old law, and the new law successively (§§ 1954–1974) but fails to show how natural law is integrated with revealed law, except to say that "the natural law provides revealed law and grace with a foundation prepared by God and attuned to the work of the Spirit" (§ 1960). Indeed, with regard to sexual ethics, the *CCC* seems to derive its norms more from natural law than from biblical morality.

There is, however, one new element in the *CCC*'s section on ethics that has won universal, though not unqualified praise, and that is its treatment of social doctrine. In its section on social justice (§§ 1928–1948), the Catechism speaks very forcefully about respect due to all human persons, about equality and differences among them, and about human solidarity. In its treatment of the seventh commandment (§§ 2401–2463), the *CCC* balances the right to private property with the universal destination of all goods. For the first time, a universal catechism prescribes respect for the integrity of creation:

> Our use of the universe's mineral, vegetable and animal resources must respect its moral dimension. Humanity's dominion over inanimate and living beings, granted by the creator, is not absolute. It must be tempered by concern for the quality of life of our neighbor, including generations to come, and calls for a religious respect for creation's integrity (§ 2415).

The Catechism links economic activity (e.g. work, economic initiative, economic life, the state, business leaders, access to jobs, just wages) to social justice. It enjoins solidarity among nations, with rich nations having "a serious moral responsibility toward nations unable by themselves to assure the means of development or impeded from doing so by tragic historical events" (§ 2439). This solidarity is carried out by direct aid and by reforming international economic and financial institutions to promote fairer relations with less advanced countries. Finally, the *CCC* speaks of the love for the poor, with those oppressed by poverty being "the object of a love of preference on the part of the church" (§ 2448).

As new and important as it is, this section on social justice is somewhat disappointing. It does not state as forcefully as it should that "action on behalf of justice and participation in the transformation of the world fully appear . . . as a constitutive dimension of the preaching of the gospel, or, in other words, of the church's mission for the redemption of the human race and its liberation from every oppressive situation."[14] Furthermore, the option for the poor is somewhat muted; it is not made into the leitmotif of the section on social justice. Indeed, this expression is not used in the *CCC.*

IV. *Christian Prayer.* Of the four parts of the Catechism, the last, on prayer, has received the most extensive revision and addition. In the provisional text, it was simply an epilogue containing a commentary on the Lord's Prayer. The definitive text elevates it into a full-fledged part and prefaces the commentary with a substantial exposition on prayer. This part is in a way a return to the *Roman Catechism:* it is divided into two sections, the first dealing with prayer in general, and the second with the Our Father.

Like the *Roman Catechism*, the first section of the fourth part offers some traditional explanations of different expressions of prayer, e.g. vocal prayer, meditation, and mental prayer (§§ 2700–2719) and practical advice on how to develop a life of prayer (§§ 2725–2745).

Unlike the *Roman Catechism*, however, the *CCC* provides a new, rich, and beautifully written exposition of prayer in the Old Testament, in the life of Jesus, and in the time of the church, with its prayers of adoration, petition, intercession, thanksgiving, and praise (§§ 2566–2649). It also emphasizes the Trinitarian structure of Christian prayer (§§ 2663–2672). Finally, it offers a brief but warm commentary on the Lord's Prayer, with its invocation ("Our Father, who art in heaven") and its seven petitions (§§ 2759–2865).

The question about what is old and what is new in the contents of the *CCC* can now be answered. There is plenty of old wine and new wine poured into the old and new skins of the *CCC*. I have highlighted only some aspects that, in my judgment, are of interest to practitioners of catechesis. Were one to follow the Lord's saying about wine and wineskins, one would wish that the *CCC* had poured the new wine into new skins. That, however, is not the case. In general, the section on Christian morality has the most old elements, that on prayer the most new elements, and those on the Creed and sacraments a fair mix of the old and the new. The question still to be considered is: What should catechists do with these elements, old and new?

## THE OLD AND THE NEW ELEMENTS IN THE *CCC* AND CATECHESIS

Every interpretation is inevitably a partial reading into the text; an interpreter brings with himself or herself a pre-understanding of which, however, he or she must be aware. Depending on their previous training and theological inclination, catechists will choose to highlight certain elements of the *CCC* rather than others. Conservatives naturally will emphasize the old elements, and liberals the new.

Catechesis, however, is not the place where one should let one's theological tendencies have a field day. As much as possible teachers of the faith must strive to transmit the whole of Christian doctrine in a unified and integrated fashion, joining faith with practice, knowledge with worship, the personal with the social. Here I would like to make some suggestions as to how the *CCC*, especially its new and old elements, should be used in catechesis.

As has been pointed out above, the Catechism is not intended to be a textbook or manual to be used directly in catechesis. Rather it is billed as "a point of reference for the catechisms or *compendia* to be composed in various countries" (§ 12). Some countries already possess their own official catechisms, while it is unlikely that countries that do not have them will be able to compose them very soon. In practice then catechists will continue to use whatever catechisms they have at their disposal.

Of course, in performing their ministry, catechists will want to consult the *CCC*. It is important, however, to note that the *CCC* is not intended to replace national and local catechisms.

Furthermore, they should not be read apart from previous official documents such as the *General Catechetical Directory,* the *Rite of Christian Initiation of Adults, To Teach as Jesus Did, Basic Teachings for Catholic Religious Education,* and *Sharing the Light of Faith.* This is vital, since there is a common danger of taking the latest official document, especially if it emanates from Rome, as the definitive and most adequate source.

In fact, in the case of the Catechism, some of its deficiencies and lacunae, which I have singled out above, can be corrected and complemented by having recourse to these other documents mentioned above. For instance, from *Sharing the Light of Faith,* it may be learned that catechesis is to be so structured that it becomes a pastoral ministry of the word to be undertaken in and through the community, a ministry that interprets experience and critically reflects on culture in order to foster the growth of faith, in intrinsic conjunction with the liturgy and for the purpose of service. Again, with regard to the contents of catechesis and their ordering, it is imperative that the *CCC* be read in light of chapter II of the *General Catechetical Directory* entitled "The More Outstanding Elements of the Christian Message."

In reference to the old and new elements of the *CCC*, it behooves catechists to understand *why* and *in what ways* they have come about. For instance, what are the consequences of adopting the four-part structure of the *Roman Catechism* for the integrity and unity of the exposition of the Christian faith and practice? What are the limitations of using the Creed as the framework for expounding Christian doctrines? What are the effects of classifying the sacramental system in analogy to the stages of human (physical) growth for sacramental theology? What are the impacts of using the decalogue as the skeleton for articulating Christian life? Finally, what shape does one give to Christian prayer if one takes the Our Father as the paradigm for all prayers? It is by examining these questions that one can come to a better appreciation of the old and new features of the *CCC* and make sense of the tensions and inadequacies that one finds in it.

Finally, we would do well to remember that "old" and "new" are relative terms, especially in matters of doctrine. Differences in terms of old and new should not therefore be hardened into oppositions, much less contradictions. In particular, with regard to Christianity, one can never prescind from the great tradition when interpreting and reformulating Christian doctrine and praxis. It is from this tradition that catechists, like the scribe who has become Christian, have to bring out both the old and the new (Mt 13:52).

# THE CATECHISM AND INTERRELIGIOUS DIALOGUE: THE JEWS AND WORLD RELIGIONS

## John Borelli

Examining the "advance copy," English edition, of the *Catechism of the Catholic Church* (December 4, 1992) and the French published edition, *Catéchisme de L'Eglise Catholique* (Mame/Phon, 1992), I have been generally encouraged by the treatment of church relations but, on a few matters, hesitant as to how certain expositions will be transposed into catechesis. Although the topic assigned to me is fairly well defined, I will give examples not only from interreligious relations but also from ecumenical relations. The staff of the Secretariat for Ecumenical and Interreligious Affairs addresses all areas of bilateral church relations and shares responsibilities for them. I focus on the work of interreligious relations beyond Catholic–Jewish relations as well as on ecumenical relations with the Byzantine Orthodox churches. Thus, it was difficult for me to study this bountiful tome in the preparation of this paper without noting how ecumenical, Jewish, and interreligious relations are all treated and offering passages to my colleagues for comment and discussion.

I was encouraged to read, in the words of Pope John Paul II ("Apostolic Constitution [*Fidei Depositum*] for the Publication of the Catechism . . ."), that the Catechism will "give support to ecumenical efforts motivated by the holy desire for the unity of all Christians, by demonstrating with precision the content and harmonious coherence of the Catholic faith." In the "Prologue" of the Catechism there is this reminder of the union of mission and ecumenism: "Those who belong to Christ through faith and baptism must confess their baptismal faith before others" (§ 14). The ecumenical movement was ushered into this century through the World Missionary Conference at Edinburgh (June 1910), at which participants realized that unity for the fulfillment of the church's mission required examination of the causes of division as well as exploration of the means for practical cooperation.

The Catechism's opening paragraph echoes the Second Vatican Council's monumental declaration on interreligious relations, *Nostra Aetate,* with the observation that God "sheds abundant light on the human search for life's ultimate meaning" (§ 26). Just two paragraphs later (§ 28), in acclaiming how "diverse peoples of the earth have expressed their quest for God . . . through their religious beliefs and behavior," the margin cross-reference is to paragraph 843, which will give a direct reference to *Nostra Aetate* and also to the Second Vatican Council's Constitution on the Church, *Lumen Gentium.*

I was pleasantly surprised to note that the last of over 3,000 references, in a text of over 2,850 numbered paragraphs and over 500 pages, is to St. Cyril of Jerusalem, whose feast is celebrated on March 18 in both the east and the west. This is a gracious reminder of the two-lung, ecumenical vision portraying the eastern church and western church working together. Having read the provisional text two years ago, I was also delighted to see a version more sensitive to inclusive language. Compare, for example, the provisional "right from his very origins, man is a *homo religiosus*" with the advance copy's "the desire for God is written on the human heart." Finally, the word "dialogue" has been incorporated throughout the present text. It most often refers to religious experience (§§ 27, 2063, 2575, 2653), but also to the ministry of Christians in the contemporary world (§§ 39, 1879), the ecumenical task for the unity of Christians (§§ 821, 1126, 1636), interreligious activity (§ 856), and sacramental celebration (§ 1153).

Other passages gave me pause and raised concerns as to how their contents will be conveyed in catechesis. One such group of passages involves the vexing usage of the term "paganism." Outside of specific reference to New Testament times (and even here I would ask for greater restriction and more precision than we have exhibited in the past), the word "pagan" and its cognates should simply not be used. Imagine the confusion of readers to find a reference to "paganism" immediately after an allusion to the tower of Babel (§ 57) and then to read in the next paragraph how the Bible honors certain great "pagans," such as Abel, Melchisedek, Noah, Daniel, and Job! Clearly the second usage approximates "Gentiles," and indeed the French edition refers to "certain great figures among the nations" (§ 58). Unfortunately, in another place the French edition lists non-believers, Jews, and pagans, while the English reads non-believers, Jews, and Gentiles (§ 498). The English follows the French later (§ 522) when describing how the messiah's coming even awakened in the hearts of pagans an obscure hope for his coming. Here "Gentile" is a more meaningful word, and "pagan" is an inappropriate translation for "Gentile." Three other references, to ancient Mediterranean mythology (§ 498) and to the writings of St. Jerome (§ 1166) and St. Justin Martyr (§ 1345), may be the only legitimate uses in the entire text, but even these are not absolutely necessary.

A larger problem looms over the use of polytheism and idolatry to explain "pagan" worship in the paragraphs on the first commandment (§§ 2112ff), because the judgment that certain acts and beliefs are polytheistic, idolatrous, or pagan often hinges on what an observer perceives others may be holding rather than what they themselves say they believe. None of the standard references in the field of history of religions discusses the term "pagan" outside of ancient Roman times and Christian literature. More often than not, the word "pagan" conveys this negative judgment and thus functions as a derogatory term. Its use should be tightly restricted.

Another example of imprecision is in the section on sacred scripture. It is stated that the Christian faith is not a "religion of the book" (§ 108) without any further reference. This sounds very close to the Quranic expression "people of the book" (*Ahl al-Kitab*), namely Jews, Christians, and others who are identified by Muslims to be in possession of scriptures. Is this a disguised challenge to those Muslims who misunderstand Christianity in this way? Probably not, but the alternative interpretation is that it is an admonition to those who take the Bible literally. In either case this is a veiled and confusing statement.

## SACRAMENTAL SHARING AND THE ONE CHURCH OF CHRIST

This topic I was not asked to do, but my responsibilities oblige me to offer a few remarks before moving to the major task. Ecumenists usually search new Catholic Church literature for two areas that have commanded their attention since the Second Vatican Council—sacramental sharing and how the teaching of "subsisted in" of *Lumen Gentium* is treated. Catholic teaching on sacramental sharing and the relation of the one church to the Catholic Church will more or less, I suggest with some trepidation, be given in the English edition with proper references to conciliar texts and the Code of Canon Law.

Regarding sacramental sharing, many necessary elements of Catholic teaching are found in §§ 1398–1401:

1) the eucharist impels Christians to unity;
2) a special relationship exists between the Catholic Church and eastern churches because the latter, through apostolic succession, have the eucharist and the priesthood;
3) eucharistic intercommunion, that is, reciprocal eucharistic sharing, with western ecclesial communities is not possible;
4) there are occasions when Catholic ministers may give the sacraments of eucharist, penance, and anointing of the sick to other [presumed "western"] Christians.

The proper texts are cited—the Second Vatican Council's Decree on Ecumenism (*Unitatis Redintegratio*) and The [1983] Code of Canon Law, c. 844, sections 3 and 4. Now one would expect a reference to the *Directory for the Application of Principles and Norms on Ecumenism* (March 25, 1993). The Code of Canons of the Eastern Churches (canon 671) is not cited, although it is word for word the same as the western canon 844. It is extremely important to note this practice for the eastern Catholic churches, which share nearly every aspect of church life and practice with the Orthodox and other ancient eastern churches.

Actually, section 3 of both canons refers to administering eucharist, penance, and anointing of the sick, without any specific condition, not only to "members of the eastern churches that do not have full communion with the Catholic Church" but also to "members of other churches, which in the judgment of the Apostolic See are in the same condition as the eastern churches as far as these sacraments are concerned." The National Conference of

Catholic Bishops received a recent judgment from the Apostolic See that the Polish National Catholic Church in the United States and Canada, a church that does not trace its origins to the reformation of the sixteenth century, falls within this category. The Catechism only refers to canon 844, section 3, and neither quotes it directly nor paraphrases it. Readers may think incorrectly that sharing these three sacraments with Orthodox Christians, and now with Polish National Catholics, must occur under the same conditions as with other Christians. This would be pastorally malapropos.

In the Catechism, "western ecclesial communities" are, in fact, described as those "derived from the reformation," but the translation of the Decree on Ecumenism is not succinct in regard to the condition of the sacraments of orders and the eucharist in these particular churches. The Catechism translates the Latin as "because they lack the sacrament of orders," but a literal translation would say "a defect in the sacrament of orders" (§ 1400). Other English translations of the official Latin text have made the same mistake. In ecumenical dialogue this view regarding orders has been under consideration.[1]

Finally, the conditions given in the Catechism (§ 1401) under which a Catholic minister of the sacrament may licitly offer the eucharist, penance, or anointing to Christians from the "reformation churches" seem to reduce the judgment of the ordinary to a case by case basis, when he, or the conference of bishops (Canon 844, 4), may prefer to state general principles. Although intercommunion, reciprocal sacramental sharing, is not possible at this time between the Catholic Church and "western ecclesial communities," there are occasions and conditions under which Catholic ministers of the sacrament may offer these three sacraments. Catechists will want to consult the newly published *Directory for the Application of Principles and Norms on Ecumenism* for propitious ways of presenting Catholic teachings on sacramental sharing (§§ 122ff).

The famous "subsisted in" passage of *Lumen Gentium* has its own surprises in the Catechism. *Lumen Gentium* 8 reads:

This church [the sole church of Christ], constituted and organized as a society in the present world, *subsists* in the Catholic Church, which is governed by the successor of Peter and by the bishops in communion with him. Nevertheless, many ele-

ments of sanctification and truth *exist* outside its visible confines
(emphases added).

This was the peculiar language employed by the Second Vatican
Council, which made a distinction between "is" and "subsists in"
and chose to say that the universal church subsists in the Catholic
Church.[2] The English advance copy gives this translation: "This
church, established and organized in this world as a society, *abides*
(*subsistit*) in the Catholic Church . . ." (§ 816) and "many elements
of sanctification and truth exist beyond the visible bounds of the
Catholic Church" (§ 819). The passages in this section add up to
a nearly accurate, if not surprisingly positive, presentation of the
ecumenical view. The "in brief" summary (§ 870) repeats this
"hymnodal" idiom "abides in." The French edition is startling by
comparison. The first presentation of the *Lumen Gentium* 8 passage comes out "this Church . . . *is realized in (subsistit in)* the Catholic Church" and "many elements of sanctification and truth exist
beyond the visible bounds of the Catholic Church." However, the
"in brief" summary completely reverses the formula: "the one
church of Christ . . . it is in the Catholic Church that it *exists* . . .
although numerous elements of sanctification and truth *subsist*
outside its structures." Was this an oversight due to the profuse-
ness of the text? Whatever it was, the French text is incorrect. Get-
ting the "subsisted in" passage correct, in line with the thinking of
the bishops at the Second Vatican Council, is hardly being pedan-
tic. At stake is conveying the expansive vision of the relationship of
other Christians to the Catholic Church.[3]

The underlying theology of degrees or levels of communion,
the gift of the Second Vatican Council to the ecumenical movement, is presented with direct references to *Lumen Gentium, Unitatis Redintegratio,* and a speech of Pope Paul VI (§ 838). Baptism is
described as "the foundation for communion among all Christians,
even those not yet in full communion with the Catholic Church"
(§ 1271), and this teaching is supportive of the Catholic view of ecumenical relations. With such a high regard for the unity already
existing among all Christians through baptism, and with other degrees of unity through the preached word, ministries in the life of
the church, etc., why are Catholics dismissing baptized candidates
from the celebration of the eucharist during their preparation for

full communion with the Catholic Church? Catechists who study these passages on degrees of communion in the Catechism will understand how objectionable such a failure to distinguish candidates from catechumens is.

The marriage of a Catholic and a baptized non-Catholic is said to mirror "the tragedy of Christian disunity" (§ 1631), and the Catechism raises up the efforts of local churches "through ecumenical dialogue" to assist them in overcoming "tensions between the spouses' obligations to each other and toward their ecclesial communities" (§ 1636). To link this widely available experience of disunity among Christians with ecumenism is pastorally effective. The recently issued revision of the ecumenical directory of the Roman Catholic Church now contains a helpful and sizeable section on mixed marriages.[4]

I missed any special reference to the more than twenty-five years of bilateral dialogues with other churches and ecclesial communities that the Catholic Church has sustained on a massive scale. References to recent agreements on christology with the Syrian and other Oriental Orthodox churches would have tempered the Catechism's presentation on monophysites (§ 467) to suggest, at least, that past disagreement does not describe present theological discourse. Reference to the fact that on December 6, 1987, the Holy Father and the patriarch of Constantinople together recited, in the original Greek without the addition of "and through the Son," the Nicene-Constantinopolitan Creed would have made the explanation of the use of *filioque* more credible (§§ 246ff). The evaluation of the differences in practice between the east and the west with regard to confirmation (§§ 1290ff) would have been improved by taking note of the wording employed by the distinguished Joint International Commission for the Theological Dialogue between the Roman Catholic Church and the Orthodox Church (Bari, 1987).

To explain justification by faith and merit, the more flexible language resulting from numerous, high level, bilateral theological dialogues was not used (§§ 1987ff). Currently, Catholic, Lutheran, Anglican, and Reformed Christians all have a number of agreements on justification by faith in various bilateral configurations. One American Lutheran bishop has described the desired next step: "the proposed interim ecumenical step of officially rescinding the contemporary applicability of mutually condemning anathemas that are as misleading as they are anachronistic for authentic church confession and mission today."[5] But perhaps the problems with the wording on justification by faith and merit and the absence of references to specific ecumenical dialogues and events in the Catechism are symptomatic of a greater dilemma—how are the churches to receive ecumenical agreements, especially through their catechesis?

## THE CATECHISM AND THE JEWS

The Catechism has done a fairly good job in not backing away from the achievements of *Nostra Aetate*. Interreligious staff at Jewish agencies were eager to have copies of the French edition as soon as it was published. This is a reminder of how profoundly significant the conciliar declaration on non-Christian religions was to Jews, coming as it did in living memory of the holocaust and at the urging of Pope John XXIII, who experienced the anguish of the Second World War's worst realities. With few adjustments the Catechism may be a positive and effective instrument in implementing recent teachings of the Catholic Church with regard to Jews. With ample specific reference to these teachings, general statements can have added meaning, for example, "Be attentive to the content and coherence of scripture as a whole" (§ 112).

The specific sections on the Jews can also be a safeguard against misunderstanding other sections, for example, the paragraphs on the stages of revelation (§§ 54ff). Paragraph 63 states that "Israel *is* the priestly people of God . . . the older brothers and sisters of all who share the faith of Abraham." The conscious choice of the present tense for the present-day people Israel determines the overall sense of the section as a whole. Hence the eschatological statement in § 60, "the people chosen to prepare for that day when God should gather all his children into the unity of the church," has meaning for Jews who are steadfast in the faith of their ancestors. Muslims also link their faith to Abraham (*Nostra Aetate* 3), and through the covenant with Noah, a gift of ancient Israel to all believers and described as a foreshadowing of the gospel (§ 58), all steadfast believers can be counted among those "in God's grace and friendship" (§ 1023).

The major section on the Jews is in the book on the Creed under the title "He suffered under Pontius Pilate, was crucified, died, and was buried" (§§ 571ff). Jesus' teaching is differentiated from that of his contemporaries (§ 574) and areas of his teaching held in common with Pharisees are also mentioned (§ 575). The paragraphs on "Jesus and the Law" use some helpful language. Whereas popular religious education materials before the Second Vatican Council tended to make a dichotomy between the two, the Catechism speaks of Jesus explaining "God's law, given on Sinai during the first covenant" and in light of the grace of the new covenant (§ 577). The authors clearly wish to avoid supersessionist language in these paragraphs, and most likely the Holy See's 1985 document, "Notes on the Correct Way To Present the Jews and Judaism in Preaching and Catechesis,"[6] was used, although no specific reference to that text is given. Similarly, while consistently holding that Jesus accomplished the law and gave it its definitive interpretation, the Catechism states that "this principle of observing the law in all its detail, not only in letter but in spirit, was dear to the Pharisees" (§ 579). This is a clear attempt to avoid the negative stereotyping of rabbinic tradition.

Any lingering notion of collective Jewish guilt, which still seems to be manifested in pageants and film, should be dispelled among Catholics in §§ 595 and 596 by discussion of division among Jewish authorities. Several cogent reasons, theological and historical, are given for not portraying the Jews as "rejected or accursed by God, as if it followed from sacred scripture" (*Nostra Aetate*, 4), with § 598 giving the clinching argument of the Catechism of Trent— "our crimes made our Lord Jesus Christ suffer the torment of the cross. . . ."

I do not want to give the impression that all of this comes out smoothly. It does not in every passage. This is an area where a high level church document, the 1985 "Notes," remains a necessary tool, since it was utilized even though not explicitly referenced. The mention in § 840 of the "tragic failure to recognize Christ Jesus" is a case in point, for the 1985 document refers to the double tragedy, as it were, of Jewish witness to God's fidelity through centuries of persecution and martyrdom.

The Christian observance of the Lord's day in relation to the sabbath is presented in §§ 2175ff. The wording of the first two sentences of § 2175 is ambiguous:

> Sunday is expressly distinguished from the sabbath, following it weekly and replacing its ceremonial observance for Christians. In Christ's passover, Sunday fulfills the spiritual truth of the Jewish sabbath and announces humanity's eternal rest in God.

What does it mean that Sunday fulfills the spiritual truth of the sabbath? Put more briefly in § 2190, the intention of these words is clearer and unfortunately more problematic: "The Jewish sabbath [happily the French edition has only 'le sabbat' at this point], recalling the completion of the first creation, has been replaced by Sunday, which recalls the new creation, inaugurated by Christ's resurrection." The sabbath precisely has not been replaced by Sunday; the sabbath is still in force for Jews. This does not conflict with the fact that "the Sunday celebration of the Lord's day and eucharist is at the heart of the church's life," that is, for Christians (§ 2176).

Other brief comments about the Catechism and the Jews would include the references to the Jewishness of Jesus and Mary (§§ 423, 439, 488, 531) and the several occasions when the reader is reminded of the Jewish roots of Christian liturgy (§§ 1096, 1226, 1340, 2175, 2767). Jews will note the condemnation of genocide as mortally sinful (§ 2313). Finally, there are places where a more accurate use of terminology shared by Jews and Christians would have been helpful. For example in § 702, Jews would have appreciated the use of "Torah" instead of "the law" when there is a clear reference to the Pentateuch.

## THE TEXT AND THE RELIGIONS

In the French edition, "religious" is indexed only for reference to the consecrated life, and so one looks up the first reference to "religion" (§ 29). The paragraph is about the suffocating tendencies of the human condition: failure, ignorance, rejection of the true and the holy, evil's omnipresence, and so on. For Buddhists this is the beginning of wisdom, but neophytes in any faith are not driven by the exceptional energies of Siddhartha Gautama. They would rather learn about the more positive features of religious experience that are presented first in the preceding paragraph:

> Throughout history and even today, the diverse peoples of the earth have expressed their quest for God in many and various ways through their religious beliefs and practices: their prayers, sacrifices, acts of worship, meditations, and so forth. These forms of religious expression, despite the ambiguities they often bring with them, are so universal that the human person can be called a religious being (§ 28).

This is followed by a paraphrase of St. Paul's sermon in Athens. A second reference to a statement by Pope John Paul II would have made this teaching thoroughly contemporary: "[God] does not fail to make himself present in many ways, not only to individuals but also to entire peoples through their spiritual riches, of which their religions are the main and essential expression . . ." (*Redemptoris Missio,* 55).

Positive references to religions can be found throughout the Catechism, but not always under the term "religion":

1) in the sections on the Creed (§§ 839ff), which amount to the major presentation of the religions;
2) in the sections on the sacraments (§ 1149): "the great religions of the world bear often impressive witness to the cosmic and symbolic meaning of religious rituals";
3) in the sections on the commandments (§ 2104): "[the duty to seek the truth, to embrace it, and hold fast to it] does not contradict a sincere respect for different religions, which frequently 'reflect a ray of the truth which enlightens everyone' . . ." (*Nostra Aetate* 2); and
4) in the sections on the "Our Father" (§ 2793): "God's concern for all people and for the whole of creation has inspired all the great practitioners of prayer and should embolden our prayer to reach the same breadth of love when we dare to say 'Our Father.'"

Certainly the Catechism is written from a broad perspective of the Catholic experience of interreligious relations over the last twenty-five years.

A general theological anthropology prevails in the text, reflected in the conciliar documents already mentioned (*Nostra Aetate* and *Lumen Gentium*) and, in addition, "The Declaration on Religious Liberty" (*Dignitatis Humanae*). Indeed the teachings of the Catholic Church on religious liberty and freedom of conscience are stated accurately (§§ 2106ff). Interreligious dialogue is called "respectful" (§ 856) and is located within the arc of elements constituting the evangelizing mission of the church (§§ 850ff.).

The major discussion of religions takes place within the explanation of the four marks of the church (one, holy, catholic, and apostolic) in §§ 811–70. It is preceded by ample discussion of the church's unity, its "woundedness" through the division among Christians, and the movement to recover unity among all Christians. Thus, this material is presented through the wondrous lens of the degrees of communion among all Christians and takes in the common ground between Jews and Christians and then the backdrop of religious experience offered to all humanity. The Catechism notes "God's gifts and calling" to Jews, which are "irrevocable (Rom 11:29)" (§ 839). Muslims, to whom Pope John Paul II has addressed major speeches over thirty times, are mentioned specifically (§ 841).

Perhaps it is not surprising that this discussion is followed by that theological conundrum with reference to St. Cyprian of Carthage: "Outside the church there is no salvation" (§§ 846ff). We are guided through it by *Lumen Gentium,* the conciliar text on mission (*Ad Gentes*), and the first reference to the encyclical marking the twenty-fifth anniversary of *Ad Gentes, Redemptoris Missio.* Christians may raise this question when they consider the extent of the church's interreligious activities and ponder reports of multireligious religious events, like the striking photo of the World Day of Prayer for Peace in Assisi (October 27, 1986).

Actually, Ignatius of Antioch may have been the first to use this admonition, but, like Cyprian, Origen before him, and others, the words were aimed at separatists and not at non-Christians. Heretics, gnostics, schismatics, and those who succumbed to apostasy under persecution were considered the opponents of the faith by these ancient fathers of the church. Hence, it is odd that the expression is introduced without the proper nuance. The "ray of truth that enlightens everyone" passage from *Nostra Aetate* will not come until much later (§ 2104), and there is no marginal cross-reference to guide the reader directly to it. The importance of interreligious dialogue will be mentioned in a few subsequent paragraphs on mission (§§ 856ff), and it is for the reader to make the connection with the foregoing section on salvation. The possibility of salvation for non-Christians is actually strongly affirmed, but documented reflections on the efficacy of other religions as means of salvation are absent.

The work of interreligious relations is transforming, and there is evidence of this in the statements of the pope. Picture if you will Christian leaders standing in an arc to the right of Pope John Paul II, beginning with Metropolitan Methodios representing Constantinople, then Dr. Robert Runcie, archbishop of Canterbury, Bishop Gabriel representing Antioch, Metropolitan Filaret of Kiev representing Moscow on around through other Orthodox and then Old Catholic and Protestant leaders, including Dr. Emilio Castro, general secretary of the World Council of Churches, and ending with Rabbi Elio Toaff and Dr. Joseph Lichten of Rome. Then, to the left of the pope, beginning with the Dalai Lama and a host of Buddhist leaders, and then extending through Islamic, Hindu and other leaders, and coming to an opposite point with traditional religious leaders from Africa and two medicine men of the Crow people from America. This picture, taken in October 1986, is worth thousands of words, but unfortunately neither the photo nor any of those words are in the Catechism.

In his address to the Roman Curia in December 1986, the pope referred to that day as the most significant event of that year and perhaps one of the most important of his pontificate. Some of those words are in *Redemptoris Missio* (§ 29) in the discussion of the work of the Holy Spirit: "Excluding any mistaken interpretation, the interreligious meeting held in Assisi was meant to confirm my conviction that every authentic prayer is prompted by the Holy Spirit, who is mysteriously present in every human heart." But this passage is not referenced in the Catechism. The reader is pointed to paragraph 55 of this encyclical (§ 846), but the eminently important sentences on the role of religions as the means by which God makes himself present to entire peoples are not quoted directly. That passage could be regarded as the first major post-conciliar clarification of the "ray of truth" phrase of *Nostra Aetate*. Finally, at the end of *Redemptoris Missio,* the pope says: "My contact with representatives of the non-Christian spiritual traditions has confirmed me in the view that the future of mission depends to a great extent on contemplation" (§ 91). These passages constitute the context of a developing Catholic understanding of relations with other believers.

Few texts of the congregations and other dicasteries of the Holy See are quoted directly in the Catechism. For example, it has already been mentioned that catechists should bear in mind the 1985 "Notes" when presenting church teachings on Jews and Judaism although this text is not cited in the Catechism. Six months after *Redemptoris Missio,* in what will be remembered as an extraordinary step in the Catholic Church's understanding of interreligious relations and dialogue, the Congregation for the Evangelization of Peoples and the Pontifical Council for Interreligious Dialogue issued jointly "Dialogue and Proclamation."[7] Coming as it did in the wake of the encyclical and citing a 1984 reflection of the Holy See's office for interreligious relations, "Dialogue and Proclamation" addresses squarely questions of mission, dialogue, and salvation.

The document recalls the often repeated fourfold typology of interreligious dialogue that has developed out of the experience of the church subsequent to the council (the dialogues of life, social action, theological exchange, and religious experience). This typology in itself provides useful explanation and encouragement to Catholics that they too can participate in one or more ways in this aspect of evangelization. This should be part of Catholic instruction on religions. Placing dialogue within the context of the evangelizing mission of the church and indicating its forms and degrees, "Dialogue and Proclamation" gives a remarkable description of how profound this work can become:

> In this dialogue of salvation, Christians and others are called to collaborate with the Spirit of the risen Lord, who is universally present and active. Interreligious dialogue does not merely aim at mutual understanding and friendly relations. It reaches a much deeper level, that of the spirit, where exchange and shar-

ing consist in a mutual witness to one's beliefs and a common exploration of one's respective religious convictions. In dialogue Christians and others are invited to deepen their religious commitment, to respond with increasing sincerity to God's personal call and gracious self-gift, which, as our faith tells us, always passes through the mediation of Jesus Christ and the work of the Spirit.

## CONCLUSION

A catechism is not expected to be on the cutting edge of theological speculation nor to reflect the solemn intuitions of church leaders and guides. Twenty years ago, a certain pessimism had settled over Catholic leadership regarding interreligious relations, particularly with Muslims. That has changed considerably by the issuance of the Catechism in the fifteenth year since the election of the most visible pope in history. Extraordinary happenings have come to pass: a public address by the head of the Catholic Church to Muslim youth in Morocco and many more addresses to Muslims afterward; the first visit by a pope to a synagogue; a gathering of many notable religious leaders to fast, walk, and listen together silently as they pray each in his own way; a letter of recognition from the Secretary-General of the Organization of the Islamic Conference to the pope for his moral leadership during the Gulf war; and much more. The twentieth century has been called by some the century of the "church" or the century of ecumenism. It might be that Catholics are only at the threshold of a century of sustained ecumenical growth and interreligious exploration.

That is the view I want to leave you with as we close this reflection upon the Catechism and interreligious relations. No single passage in this large volume should be taken alone, particularly in regard to interreligious understanding. There are references throughout the text to religions and interreligious relations. They add up to a still developing picture to which even the church documents cited and related current documents bear witness. Overall this is a very positive view, solidly founded on the teachings and experience of Catholics, and still opening up possibilities for spiritual growth and understanding.

# LITURGICAL CATECHESIS ACCORDING TO THE CATECHISM

## Catherine Dooley

Liturgical catechesis in the framework of catechisms is unique to the *Catechism of the Catholic Church (CCC)*. In fact the introduction of both the term "liturgical catechesis" and the endeavor itself is a relatively new catechetical development in the United States.[1] In the *CCC,* liturgical catechesis is described as mystagogy: a means of initiating "people into Christ's mystery by moving from the visible to the invisible, from the sign to the thing signified, from the sacraments to the mystery they represent" (§ 1075).[2] This essay will look at the overall framework of the *CCC* in order to see the context of liturgical catechesis and then examine Book Two (The Celebration of the Christian Mystery) for an understanding of liturgical catechesis in the *CCC.*

### STRUCTURE OF THE *CATECHISM OF THE CATHOLIC CHURCH*

The *Catechism of the Catholic Church* is divided into four books, structured around the "four pillars": creed, sacraments, commandments, and prayer. The ordering of the four pillars of the *CCC* is significant because the organization of the content in itself presents a catechetical message. These four pillars reflect the unity of faith of the early church and offer a holistic approach to catechesis.[3] The Christian mystery expressed in the Creed is celebrated in liturgical action; lived out, enlightened, and supported by the commandments; and deepened by prayer, particularly the Our Father. The sacraments are encounters with the living God who again is actively present in the lives of people, the same God active in creation, covenant, and exodus. The sacraments are not things; they are a relationship with the God who has first loved us.

The ordering of the *CCC* follows the structure of the *Cate-*

*chism of the Council of Trent* (*Roman Catechism*) and differs from catechisms of the recent past such as the *Baltimore Catechism.* The *Baltimore Catechism* used Creed, commandments, sacraments, and prayer as its sequence.[4] In the *Baltimore Catechism* schema the commandments are the focus of the Christian life and sacraments are seen as a means of grace that strengthen Christians to live the moral life and fulfill the obligations imposed. The various editions of the *Baltimore Catechism* used different illustrations to convey this point. One image was a train (soul) on the road to heaven refueled and energized by the seven powerhouses (sacraments). This view presents sacraments as channels of grace by which individuals became holy. Sacraments are things, like a battery that recharges. In fact, in the 1917 Code of Canon Law, the sacraments were listed under the heading of "*de rebus* (on things)."[5] Each sacrament was defined in terms of sign, matter and form, and cause and effect in order to explain its nature and function. On an academic level or in seminaries, sacramental theology and liturgy were two distinct endeavors that have only recently been integrated.[6]

Another image of the sacraments used in the *Baltimore Catechism* is the parallel between aspects of individual life and spiritual life, i.e. birth–baptism; adulthood–confirmation; food–eucharist; medicine–penance.[7] The *Catechism of the Catholic Church* continues to use the analogy of human growth as a broad framework for understanding the sacraments, but the purpose of the *CCC* arrangement is to show the sacraments as an organic whole in which each sacrament has its own vital place. The sacraments are divided into sacraments of initiation (baptism, confirmation, and eucharist); sacraments of healing (penance and anointing of the sick); and sacraments in service of communion (marriage and holy orders). The sacraments touch all the stages and important moments of Christian life and resemble those of natural life.

The Catechism states that there are other ways of ordering the sacraments than this threefold division and affirms that the "eucharist, the sacrament of sacraments, holds an unique place in this whole and all other sacraments are ordered to it as their end" (§ 1211). Yet the only place in which there is a full treatment of the eucharist is in the section on the sacraments of initiation. In the light of the whole of Book Two, the analogy of human growth as an organizing framework stunts the organic approach to the sacraments as ecclesial sacraments, actions of the church, "the sacrament of Christ's action, at work through the mission of the Holy Spirit" (§ 1118), and gives the impression that the sacraments are all equal. The New Testament is clear that baptism and eucharist are fundamental to the whole sacramental system and that the other sacraments draw their meaning from their relationship to baptism and eucharist.[8] Using the analogy of human growth counters the rich description of the common elements of sacraments in paragraphs 1113 to 1130 of the *CCC.*

## LITURGICAL CATECHESIS

The discussion of liturgical catechesis is located in Book Two, "The Celebration of the Christian Mystery," which has two parts: "The Sacramental Economy" and "The Seven Sacraments." These two sections are preceded by a short introduction on the meaning of liturgy. That the sacraments are placed squarely in the context of liturgy seems obvious, but it is unique with regard to the content of catechisms and reflects the liturgical reform of Vatican II.

The *CCC* emphasizes that the liturgy is "the privileged place for catechizing the people of God" (§ 1074), and liturgical catechesis endeavors to initiate people into the mystery of Christ by proceeding from the visible to the invisible, from the sign to the thing signified, from the sacrament to the mysteries they represent" (§ 1075). According to the *CCC,* liturgical catechesis and mystagogy are synonymous.[9]

The *CCC* gives an outline of the elements of liturgical catechesis. First, liturgical catechesis implies an understanding of the sacramental economy (§ 1135). Second, catechesis should help the faithful to open themselves to a spiritual understanding of the economy of salvation as the liturgy reveals it and enables them to live it out (§ 1095). Third, fundamental catechesis on the sacramental celebrations will respond to the first questions posed by the faithful on this subject:

— who celebrates?
— how do we celebrate?
— when do we celebrate?
— where do we celebrate? (§ 1135)

## SACRAMENTAL ECONOMY

Sacramental economy is the focus of the first part of Book Two. Economy is a "theological term used to refer to God's activity in the world, particularly with reference to the two dispensations of Old Testament and New Testament."[10] The economy of salvation is God's saving plan revealed in creation, covenant, exodus and passover, the prophets, in the person and works of Jesus Christ, and in the age of the church. In the sacramental economy Christ present in the power of the Spirit "reveals, makes present and communicates his work of salvation through the liturgy of the church until he comes again" (§ 1076). Liturgy therefore is the work of the Trinity. Christian worship arises out of a Trinitarian understanding of salvation and is therefore christological and paschal. The *CCC* underlines the paschal mystery as the center of the entire liturgy. The paschal mystery is the heart of the liturgical year and it is the paradigm for the Christian life. "Christ signifies and makes present his paschal mystery primarily through the church's liturgy" (§ 1085). To accomplish so great a work, Christ is always present to his church, especially in liturgical celebrations (§ 1088). Christ is present in the church in the assembly gathered, in the person of the minister presiding, in the word proclaimed, and in the eucharistic bread and wine blessed and broken for us. This mystery of Christ is made present and real by the transforming power of the Spirit. When the Spirit encounters the response of faith that he awakens in us, then the liturgy becomes the common work of the Holy Spirit and the church. In the Spirit the church is united to Christ's life and mission.

Throughout this section on sacramental economy, several strong themes emerge. These are the consistent interrelationship of the Old and New Testaments, the continuity of the saving action of God with the liturgical action, and the gift and action of the Spirit that underlies the whole catechesis of sacrament, particularly the unifying and transforming power of the Spirit within the body of Christ.

## SPIRITUAL UNDERSTANDING AND TYPOLOGY

The second principle of liturgical catechesis in the *CCC* is that catechesis should help the faithful to open themselves to a spiritual understanding of the economy of salvation as the liturgy reveals it and enables us to live it out. This section is crucial for an understanding of sacrament and liturgical catechesis in the *CCC*. The "spiritual understanding," one of the aims of liturgical catechesis, is linked to the unity of the two Testaments through typology, which sees in God's works of the old covenant prefigurations of what God would accomplish in the fullness of time, in the person of God's incarnate Son (§ 128).

The *CCC* proposes the paschal catechesis of the risen Christ on the road to Emmaus as the model for catechesis, particularly with regard to the harmony of the two Testaments, and notes that this same approach to catechesis was also used by the apostles and fathers of the church (§ 1094). Just as the risen Christ helped the disciples to understand the mystery of his death pre-figured in the old covenant and to recognize him in the breaking of the bread, so the Holy Spirit "recalls and reveals Christ to the faith of the assembly" (§ 1092). Catechesis uncovers the mystery of Christ through those types—persons, places, things or events—that identify patterns of God's gracious activity in history which enable us to remember and, in remembering, to see God revealed in the present moment and as future hope. Events like the flood and the water from the rock are a type of baptism; Moses is a type for Jesus. "Manna in the desert pre-figured the eucharist, the bread that comes down from heaven" (§ 1094). For this reason, the church, especially during Advent and Lent and above all at the Easter vigil, rereads and relives the great events of salvation history in the "today" of its liturgy.

Typology, as an approach to scripture, is widely used throughout the Catechism. It is defined in the *CCC* as the discernment "in God's works of the old covenant pre-figurations of what he would accomplish in the fullness of time, in the person of his incarnate Son" (§ 128). The text asserts that Christians read the Old Testament in the light of the paschal mystery. "Such typological reading discloses the inexhaustible content of the Old Testament, which does not allow us to forget that it retains its own value as revelation, as our Lord reaffirmed. In addition the New Testament must be read in the light of the Old" (§ 129). "It is a method by which interpreters attempt to go beyond the literal sense of a passage to a "'more-than-literal' or symbolic sense."[11] Certain criteria exist with regard to typology. Types (persons, places, things, or events) must be written of in the scriptures. Types foreshadow the future, but Raymond Brown emphasizes that the type "is silhouette not a portrait of the antitype. The relationship between type and antitype is always imperfect."[12] Moreover, authentic typology is always related to God's plan of salvation and to an emphasis on promise/fulfillment.

In the *Catechism of the Catholic Church,* mystagogy and typology are intertwined. In the sections that deal with each individual sacrament, the sacrament is placed within the economy of salvation and connected to prefigurations of the sacrament in the first covenant. While the *CCC* discusses the stages in the formation of the gospels (§§ 125–126) and insists that "literary forms used in the Bible should be taken into account in interpreting scripture," it consistently fails to do so in its own text.[13] As Mary Boys noted in her critique of the preliminary draft of the *CCC,* "It is curious that typology should figure so prominently in the catechism when earlier ecclesial documents point to its problematic character."[14] The *CCC* looks to the preaching of the fathers of the church as the paradigm for mystagogy, but even in the patristic era, typology had its problems. The most obvious of these is the venomous anti-semitism that often accompanied the patristic interpretation of the scriptures. When the church fathers used this methodology of typology they did not always distinguish between types/antitypes and allegory, in which every element in a story is given another symbolic meaning in a one-to-one correspondence. Their interpretation of the scripture sometimes distorted the original meaning of the passage by imposing a creative "spiritual sense."

In fact, Enrico Mazza states that if we ask why mystagogical catechesis and mystagogical commentary have for all practical purposes disappeared from the contemporary Roman church, it is because allegory has historically been the death of mystagogy.[15] Even modern authors, however, who have attempted to distinguish between allegory and typology by stating that typology is based on historical connection while allegory is purely imaginative, have found the distinction "simplistic and an overstatement."[16] With the introduction of the historical critical method and a renewed interest in hermeneutics in the nineteenth and early twentieth century, typology remained an issue of debate among some scholars but in general, modern scripture study does not make much use of typology.

Typology is an issue raised by the scriptural approach of the Catechism, but other concerns, such as the relationship of Christianity and Judaism, the revision of the lectionary,[17] a more-than-literal interpretation of the scriptures, lectionary-based catechesis, and an RCIA-inspired emphasis on mystagogy also demand that the question of typology be studied further.[18]

With regard to the lectionary, some contemporary critics charge that the use of typology in the lectionary does not respect the integrity of the Old Testament and obscures the fact that the Old Testament is a revelation of God in its own right.[19] Moreover, some authors posit that this harmonizing of Old Testament readings in the lectionary with the gospels leads to an anti-semitism.[20] Another major concern is that types will be proposed without any basis in actual events or in the intentions of the authors, thereby ignoring historical-critical exegesis. These are serious charges.

In response to these concerns, some scholars point out that the method of typology was frequently used by the New Testament writers to express the unity of scripture and of God's plan.[21] For example, in the letter to the Romans, Adam is seen as a type of Christ, who is thus the antitype. The exodus is a type of baptism in First Corinthians (10:2), and Matthew uses the image of Moses to paint his picture of Jesus. In the same vein, in response to the charge that the promise/fulfillment themes of the lectionary needlessly constrain the biblical message and leave delicate issues wide open to serious misinterpretation, "it may be broadly stated that the sort of prediction-fulfillment schema involved in the liturgical use of the OT texts does not differ appreciably from much of the NT use of the OT."[22]

Secondly, no typological interpretation of scripture can legitimately be given to a text unless it is related to the literal meaning of the text—"literal" meaning the sense that the author directly intended and that the written words conveyed. In other words, for its own integrity and for the prevention of possible misinterpretation, typology needs the checks and balances of historical-critical methodology.[23]

Thirdly, the language of the Christian liturgy is filled with typological references, and this linguistic and symbolic heritage is the medium for retelling and continuing the story of salvation. Unfortunately a lack of biblical literacy on the part of many Catholics renders the connections unintelligible[24] and the literalism to which we have been educated "has become a prevailing and unexamined habit of mind."[25] The *CCC* uses the blessing of the baptismal water at the Easter vigil as an example of the use of typology in mystagogy but it is also a good description of the current situation. In the prayer, the Old Testament images are seen as types of baptism and are fulfilled in Christ and the church. On the one hand this is a good illustration because it indicates that no one image can adequately express the meaning of baptism and it places baptism in continuity with the saving power present since the beginning of time. On the other hand, instead of allowing the images to speak to the imagination, the prayer is preoccupied with explaining and explicitating the meaning, e.g. "The waters of the great flood you made a sign of the waters of baptism. . . ."

Perhaps the Catechism is calling for the same thing as many liturgists, scripture scholars, and catechists today: a restoration of a biblical heritage to believers. In patristic times people were steeped in those passages that were read to them from the scriptures and that were expounded upon in the homilies. The images of the scriptures were part and parcel of the language of the homilist and the hearer. In our modern terminology we might call that "biblical literacy." The *CCC* is proposing that typology is a way to illustrate the intrinsic connection between the Testaments. God's revelation in the Old Testament continues in the New. The story needs to be known from beginning to end because the New Testament cannot be understood except in reference to the Old.

Clearly, typology holds an important place within the *CCC* but not as a topic in and of itself. Typology is seen as an expression of the unity of the Old and New Testaments, but the *CCC,* by placing typology in the context of mystagogy, seems to be offering to the faithful a way of understanding the action of God in terms of their own life. The presentation of biblical types does not aim to restore the old salvation history approach nor does it limit the meaning of the sacraments. Rather it seems to be a way of exploring a wide variety of biblical images and associations evoked by ritual and prayer in the light of God's saving action in history and in the context of the believer's day-to-day life. A rethinking of typology has interesting possibilities in the context of liturgical catechesis (mystagogy) in new cultural situations, but the *CCC* does not offer much in the way of guidance to catechists as to how typology is to be used in mystagogical catechesis. This is a major question and challenge of Book Two of the *Catechism of the Catholic Church.*

## COMMON ELEMENTS OF THE CHURCH'S SACRAMENTS

The third element in the *CCC* for liturgical catechesis is that fundamental catechesis on the sacramental celebrations will respond to the first questions posed by the faithful on the subject (§ 1135): Who celebrates? How do we celebrate? When do we celebrate? Where do we celebrate? Using these questions as a framework, this chapter of the *CCC* describes the common elements in the celebration of the church's sacraments. The whole section is a fine exposition of parts of the Constitution on the Sacred Liturgy. The Catechism again places the treatment of each of the sacraments individually within a liturgical context. It is at this point that there seems to be a shift in perspective. The Catechism describes mystagogy as "initiation into Christ's mystery, proceeding from the visible to the invisible, from the sign to the thing signified, from the sacrament to the mysteries they represent" (§ 1075). In the treatment of the individual sacraments, however, the sacramental celebration is not taken as the starting point of catechesis as in the mystagogical catechesis of the early church, where the articulation of the meaning of the sacrament was evoked by the experience of the liturgy.[26] Rather the starting point in the Catechism is the doctrinal teaching of the church derived primarily from the revised Code of Canon Law. There are minimal references to the sacramental rites and little indication that the theology of the introduction, the signs, actions and prayers are used as a source. This is not to diminish the Code. The canons of the Code on the sacraments have been revised in light of the liturgical books or are derived from them. I am only saying that the Code is not the starting point for mystagogy and that the Code must be read in the context of the liturgical books in order to provide interpretative background or a rationale for the law.[27]

The discussion of each of the sacraments follows the same

pattern. The first article treats the name and the nature of the sacrament. The next article places the sacrament within the economy of salvation in order to show how the sacrament was pre-figured in the Old Testament and to reinforce the unity of the two Testaments. The ritual celebration itself is discussed and an explanation is given of the symbols and symbolic actions. This is named, at least in the articles on baptism, "the mystagogy of celebration," which reduces mystagogy to explanation. The next sections deal with who is the recipient, who is the minister, and what is the effect of the sacrament. The discussion of each sacrament is diminished by a lack of attention to the historical background and evolution of the sacrament.

All in all, the presentation of the theology of the individual sacraments is uneven. Despite a good section on common elements of sacramental celebrations that emphasizes the importance of the assembly and the Holy Spirit at work in the church through the sacraments, the material on individual sacraments gives a minimal role to the assembly or the Holy Spirit in the celebration. The continuity with the Old Testament and the early church is a strong theme throughout the presentation of the sacraments. An attempt is made to show the relationship of liturgy and justice— for example, the statement that "the eucharist directs our concern toward the poor" (§ 1397).

As far as pastoral questions are concerned, there are no ready answers. For example, with regard to the current discussion on the sequence of the sacraments of initiation the text does not resolve the dispute. Rather, acknowledging the current practice of infant baptism in the Roman rite, it seems to favor a restoration of the sequence of baptism, confirmation, and eucharist, even though these sacraments are separated by a number of years: "the baptism of infants is followed by years of catechesis before being completed by confirmation and the eucharist, the summit of Christian initiation" (§ 1233). The text endorses the catechumenate as the means of Christian initiation (§ 1230) and states that the Christian initiation of adults begins with their entrance into the catechumenate and culminates in the celebration of the three sacraments of initiation: baptism, confirmation, and eucharist. In baptizing children the stages of initiation are abridged, therefore, providing the need for a post-baptismal catechumenate (§1231).

With regard to the Christian faith and "other religions" the Catechism affirms that the "church does not know of any means other than baptism that assures entrance into eternal happiness. For this reason, it has not neglected the mission it received from the Lord to enable all who can be baptized to 'be reborn of water and Spirit.' God has linked salvation to the sacrament of baptism but he is not bound to his sacraments" (§ 1257).

The articles on the age for confirmation, like the current practice, represent an ambiguous area. In the section on the recipient of the sacrament of confirmation, the *CCC* affirms that all baptized persons not yet confirmed can and should receive the sacrament of confirmation (§ 1306). It then states that the Latin tradition holds that "the age of discretion is the time for baptized children to receive confirmation. But in danger of death children should be confirmed even if they have not yet attained the age of discretion" (§ 1307). The articles refer to canon 891. Since this canon is read in terms of the *Roman Pontifical,* which allows conferences of bishops to determine a suitable age, it does not seem that these articles mean much in terms of a moving toward a uniformity of practice.

What is clear, however, is that at whatever age confirmation is celebrated, it is to be understood in relationship to the baptismal commitment: ". . . in the Roman Rite in the case of children baptized in infancy, the liturgy of confirmation . . . begins with the renewal of baptismal promises and the profession of faith on the part of the confirmands. It thus reveals clearly that confirmation follows in the wake of baptism" (§ 1298).

**THE AIM OF THE CATECHISM**

A catechism is a specific genre of writing. It is not a liturgical book and it is necessary to keep its purpose in mind. The aim of the Catechism is "to serve the whole church in the diversity of its rites and its cultures, and to present what is fundamental and common to the whole church concerning the liturgy as mystery and as celebration, then the sacraments and sacramentals" (§ 1075). The concept of liturgical catechesis (mystagogy) is unique to this catechism and offers a direction that will prove to be challenging to catechists. Placing the sacraments in the context of liturgy is unparalleled in a catechism. Yet this is only a toehold as far as understanding and fostering liturgical catechesis. The Catechism quotes the Constitution on the Sacred Liturgy, but the spirit of that document is largely missing. Perhaps the good result will be that catechists and liturgists will work together to offer a clear understanding of the meaning of liturgical catechesis. The doctrinal approach of Book Two on the celebration of the Christian mysteries can only be read in the light of the *Roman Pontifical* and the book of rites. "The challenge of a contemporary mystagogy on sacrament remains to be taken up."[28]

Moreover, by itself the *CCC* cannot carry the burden of a renewal of catechesis in today's church. It has to be supported by the awareness that our faith is the faith of the church, by a conversion of heart of the pastoral leaders who are called upon to implement the Catechism, by serious scripture study, by a recognition of the need to celebrate well so that the liturgy can exercise its inherent power, and by the efforts to continually work for justice; in brief, by enabling the community to recognize and live its identity and mission.

# THE FORMATION OF CONSCIENCE ACCORDING TO THE CATECHISM

## Robert M. Friday

If this essay were to focus exclusively on what the Catechism says about "the formation of conscience," it would be very brief, indeed! In the Catechism, Book Three, entitled "Life in Christ," treats the subject of moral conscience in Article 6 and, within that context, devotes three numbered paragraphs to "the formation of conscience." The brevity of this treatment ought not to suggest that formation of personal conscience is taken lightly by the Catechism, or (and this would be even more problematic) that conscience formation is a relatively minor ingredient in the Christian's moral formation. In fact, a thoughtful, attentive reading of these three paragraphs should confirm our suspicion that an investigation into conscience and its formation will necessitate a much broader consideration of (1) the nature of the Christian moral life itself, (2) the phenomenon of moral decision-making, and (3) the development of individual moral character, which is the penultimate goal of conscience formation.

### CONSCIENCE: PAST AND PRESENT

Allow me to note that whereas "conscience" as a term has been with us for much of our tradition as a Christian people, its nature, role in decision-making and character development, formation, and authority have not received much attention within the traditional catechisms. The *Baltimore Catechism No. 3* (1949 revised edition), for example, in Lesson 29 on penance, urges the sinner who would be repentant to examine his or her conscience, and then proceeds to describe how to go about such an examination in preparation for confession. However, nowhere in the *Baltimore Catechism* is conscience ever defined or described. The faithful were expected simply to have formed a right and honest conscience, whatever it is, which was to guide them in their decision-making. My own personal parochial school recollection of the nature and content of "conscience formation" suggests that we were to learn well the commandments of God and of the church and, when in doubt, simply and unquestionably to do what the church (pope, bishop, priests, and sisters) tells us to do. Much of the more nuanced theological tradition of the teaching church on the issue of conscience, contained in the moral manuals, never made it to the pews and classrooms of St. Phillip's Church in Pittsburgh, PA.

Vatican Council II, where "conscience" surfaces prominently in such documents as *Gaudium et spes* (GS) and *Dignitatis humanae* (DH), spurred greater interest, and sometimes confusion, in the matter of personal conscience. The latter document, especially, with its strong assertion regarding the authority and autonomy of conscience in matters religious, was liberating for some, terribly unsettling for others, especially for those whose pursuit of beatitude was driven by the *Baltimore Catechism*. Listen to the Declaration on Religious Liberty:

> The Vatican Council declares that the human person has a right to religious freedom. Freedom of this kind means that all men should be immune from coercion on the part of individuals, social groups and every human power so that, within due limits, nobody is forced to act against his convictions in religious matters in private or in public, alone or in associations with others (DH 2).

> It is through his conscience that man sees and recognizes the demands of the divine law. He is bound to follow this conscience faithfully in all his activity so that he may come to God, who is his last end. Therefore he must not be forced to act contrary to his conscience. Nor must he be prevented from acting according to his conscience, especially in matters religious (DH 3).[1]

This stance toward freedom in following one's conscience—rather than simply obeying church teaching, if personal conscience and church teaching are in conflict—in regard to what one believes about God, and the implications of that belief for one's "fundamental option" and daily life, was something of a reversal to the

stance taken at Vatican Council I. Regardless, the notion of conscience as the ultimate subjective authority in moral decision-making
was and is fundamental to our tradition as reiterated through the
ages.

## AUTONOMY OF PERSONAL CONSCIENCE: BALANCE NEEDED

The institutional church's concern since Vatican II often has
been with the way conscience has been highlighted in more recent moral theory and practice. Appeals to "my conscience" have
to a great extent replaced appeals to "what the church teaches" in
the moral vocabulary and lives of many Catholics. While there is a
theological correctness to the conscience appeal, there is also cause
for some concern, a concern often voiced by church leaders, who
perceive a growing disregard for "the sacred and certain teaching
of the church" (DH 14). The Catechism reflects this concern (e.g.
§ 1792).[2] At the core of the concern is the question of conscience
formation. How does the human conscience assimilate the values
that fund moral decisions? From what sources are these values
learned? At what age and with what degree of endurance? And
where do the authoritative teachings of the magisterium fit into the
enterprise of conscience formation? The Catechism will not directly
address each of these questions, but it will provide insight and guidance for all who struggle with them, especially for those who are
to help others with the struggle, i.e. bishops and catechists.

In assessing and critiquing the Catechism's portrayal of conscience formation, it is necessary to note that the document's
overall ecclesiology (including the role and authority of the magisterium[3]) and its vision of what constitutes the believer's "life in
Christ" (the moral life) is rather key. "Key" though these elements
are, an in-depth analysis of each is beyond the scope of this paper.
Other presenters have addressed some of these issues, and commentators in future months will dig more deeply, I'm sure. My point
in noting this is simply that, if conscience is to be formed, there
must be some desired end or goal that dictates the shape and the
content of the formation. What values are to mark my life so that
I live according to the gospel? What does "life in Christ" look like?
What stance counts as "loving" in the face of our national health

care problems, or the abortion issue, the situation in Bosnia, and the environmental concerns plaguing modern society?

## THE MORAL VISION OF THE CATECHISM

Following a traditional catechism format, Book One of the new Catechism describes, within the framework of the Christian Creed, the realities of God and humankind, and the nature of the relationship (loving) between them. Jesus Christ is presented not only as redeemer-savior, but also as the model for the life to be lived by believers who are, in the words of St. Paul, to "put on Christ" who is the way, the truth, and the light. Those who respond to the call to follow Christ constitute the church, which has its earthly, structured and hierarchical reality.

Book Two addresses the liturgical and sacramental life of the church. The treatment of the sacraments is largely traditional, although the communal dimension of each sacrament, following the impetus and correctives of Vatican II, receives greater emphasis, e.g. the effect of baptism as an initiation into the faith community rather than simply the removal of original sin. The overall perception is that the life of the Christian is life in community, with all of its privileges and responsibilities. In the community of believers we are to encounter our God and learn gospel values, and other community members are to encounter Christ in us.

Perhaps I expected as a natural outgrowth of this vision of church and Christian life that Book Three, which treats morality, would reflect a greater emphasis on loving response in personal relationships with God, self, neighbor, and world. In fact, adherence to law, specifically to the decalogue, still appears to be the measure of the Christian moral life. Describing Christian moral behavior within the framework of the ten commandments is familiar (cf. the *Baltimore Catechism*) and traditional. It also suggests that "sin" will be presented in terms of law breaking and "conscience formation" in terms of learning the details of law as the expectation of God for God's people. The goal envisioned for the Christian man and woman is that they be persons who know and keep the law.

In fairness to the Catechism, "law" is not equated exclusively or totally with the decalogue. The "law of love" commanded by Jesus is certainly and prominently acknowledged: "The law of the gospel is expressed most profoundly in Jesus' new commandment 'Just as I have loved you, you also should love one another'" (§ 1970).

This scriptural passage from John 15:12 is considered by many contemporary Catholic moral theologians to be the cornerstone for Christian ethics. It distinguishes the new covenant ethic from the ethic of the former covenant in that it offers not law as the standard, but the person of Jesus Christ. This passage is the biblical tool most used to extricate us from the legalistic thrust of the pre-Vatican II morality, the roots of which stretch back to the penitential books of the sixth and seventh centuries.

After citing this Johannine passage, the Catechism goes on at this point to further emphasize the centrality of love in the Christian life.

> ". . . Let love be genuine. . . . Love one another with mutual affection. . . . Rejoice in hope, be patient in suffering, persevere in prayer. Contribute to the needs of the saints; extend hospitality to strangers." This catechesis [Romans] teaches us also to treat cases of conscience in the light of our relationship to Christ and the church (§ 1971).

> The new law is called a law of love because in place of fear it substitutes the love poured out by the Holy Spirit as the motive for our actions; a law of grace, because by means of faith and the sacraments it imparts the grace that makes it possible to act; a law of freedom, because it sets us free from the ritual and juridical observances of the old law, inclines us to act spontaneously under the impetus of love and, finally, leads us from the state of servants who do "not know what the master is doing" to that of Christ's friends, "because I have made known to you everything that I have heard from my Father," and even to the status of God's children and heirs (§ 1972).

Curiously, I believe, the Catechism, despite the above statements, betrays an ambivalence in choosing between the law of "law" and the law of "love" in developing its moral base. For example, in the section under Conscience dealing with making right choices, the Catechism notes some rules that it maintains apply in every instance. One of the rules cited is "the golden rule": "In everything do to others what you would have them do to you; for this is the law and the prophets" (Mt 7:12).[4] The golden rule, I submit, which offers one's own likes and dislikes as an ethical measure, a kind of "self-standard ethics," falls short of the law of the gospel, which in paraphrase says, "In everything do to others *as Christ has done to you.*"

## THE PHENOMENON OF SIN

Building on this commanding invitation "to love as Christ loves" as the basis for Christian morality, many contemporary moralists contend that appropriate response in and to love relationships with God, self, neighbor, and cosmos is the measure of life in Christ. The essence of "grace" is that of an enduring love relationship, a state of being, with the four objects named. "Sin," then, formally understood, is also a state of being rather than an action, a state of being marred by broken relationship and alienation. "Sins," if we might speak of such, are those thoughts, desires, words, deeds, or omissions which signify and symbolize that state of brokenness. Although lists or examples of potentially sinful signs can be constructed relative to each of the four relationships, the focus will remain on the "response to loving relationship" rather than on the concrete "willful thought, desire, word, action, or omission forbidden by the law of God," as sin is defined in q. 64 of the *Baltimore Catechism.* The prohibitions of the decalogue in much of contemporary moral theology serve as expressions of what sin (unlovingness) looks like rather than as blueprints for living the Christian life. In the Catechism the ten commandments appear to be the blueprint.

Sin, in the Catechism, "is an offense against reason, truth and right conscience, a failure of authentic love for God and neighbor caused by a disordered attachment to certain goods" (§ 1849). Using the words of both Augustine and Thomas, it is "an act, a word or a desire contrary to the eternal law" (§ 1849).

The Catechism, however, does not attribute "sin" to the agent wholly on the basis of the physical act, but is quite clear on the traditional requirement for there being full knowledge and complete consent.

> For a sin to be mortal, three conditions must be met: "Mortal sin is sin whose object is grave matter and which is also com-

mitted with full knowledge and deliberate consent" (*Reconcili-atio et poenitentia*, 17) (§ 1857).

Mortal sin requires full knowledge and complete consent. It presupposes knowledge of the sinful character of the act, of its opposition to God's law, and implies a consent sufficiently deliberate to be a personal choice. Feigned ignorance and hardening of the heart do not diminish, but rather increase, a sin's voluntary character (§ 1859).

Accordingly, the document acknowledges that "although we can judge that an act is in itself a serious offense, we must entrust the judgment of persons to the justice and mercy of God" (§ 1861).

Anyone schooled in certain contemporary approaches to "doing" moral theology (e.g. according to Richard McCormick S.J., Charles Curran, Richard Gula, Timothy O'Connell) will find the Catechism's treatment of morality in Book Three something closer to that of the moral manualist tradition. It is predominantly act- and law-centered, especially in regard to personal ethics. The notion of certain actions being "intrinsic evils" is certainly and emphatically retained (e.g. masturbation [§ 2352], homosexual acts [§ 2357], contraceptive acts [§ 2370]). However, it must be admitted that any departure from this designation would have been a rather significant, and unexpected, change.

While the terms are not directly used, the traditional distinction between "objective" and "subjective" when speaking of human acts is generally and, in my judgment, usefully maintained when speaking of an action being "evil" rather than "sinful." With some exceptions,[5] objective acts are labeled serious moral evils or serious offenses rather than the more subjective, and judgmental, "sins." It has been neither theologically correct nor pastorally advantageous to term objective actions such as abortion, contraception, and homosexual acts as "sins."

Up to this point I have attempted to provide a sense of the moral theology at work in the *Catechism of the Catholic Church* by contrasting it to what I believe has been the general thrust of much of the contemporary moral theology that has found its way into mainstream catechetical materials. Against that backdrop, I wish now to focus attention specifically on the issue of moral conscience and conscience formation as encountered in the Catechism.

## CONSCIENCE: NATURE, AUTHORITY, AND FORMATION

The Catechism calls us toward life in Christ marked by the dual command to obey the ten commandments and to "love as Christ loves." While the former may suggest a life characterized by conformity and obedience, the latter suggests reasonable, free, and holistic response to the sometimes individualized demands of a loving relationship. The attempt to accommodate and harmoniously collate both approaches may prove conflictual, especially at the level of conscience.

## THE NATURE OF CONSCIENCE

The Catechism, in § 1776, turns to the Pastoral Constitution on the Church in the Modern World for its description of conscience:

> In the depths of his conscience, man detects a law which he does not impose upon himself, but which holds him to obedience. Always summoning him to love good and avoid evil, the voice of conscience can, when necessary, speak to his heart more specifically: do this, shun that. For man has in his heart a law written by God. To obey it is the very dignity of man; according to it he will be judged. *Conscience is the most secret core and sanctuary of a man. There he is alone with God, whose voice echoes in his depths* (emphasis mine) (GS, 16).

The Catechism acknowledges that every person has a conscience that, in a general way, inclines him or her to do good and to avoid evil. In the face of specific choices the moral conscience approves good actions and denounces evil actions. Reflecting St. Thomas, the Catechism maintains that the nature of love is to desire in our choices good for someone.[6] Conscience is so integral to human nature that the demands of natural law are knowable by "prudent people," but may, because of original sin, need to be revealed in, for example, codes such as the decalogue. Thus, if one were simply to listen carefully and openly to the voice of conscience, one would naturally be drawn toward the truth. In this understanding, "moral conscience is a judgment of reason by which a human person perceives the moral quality of a specific act which he or she intends, is in the process of doing or has already done" (§ 1778).

The dignity of the human person implies and requires up-rightness of moral conscience, which includes: the perception of the *principles of morality* (*synderesis*[7]); their *application* in the given circumstances by practical discernment between princi-ples and values; and *judgment* about concrete acts already done or yet to be done. The *prudent judgment* of conscience recog-nizes practically and concretely the truth about the moral good, declared by the law of reason. The person who chooses in keeping with this judgment is called prudent (§ 1780).[8]

Moral theologians point out that the activity of conscience goes beyond simply making immediate choices. It also contributes determinatively to the formation of our moral character, the kind of person we are and are becoming, because imbedded in and underlying our choices are the values that shape our lives. Our choices are the windows into the deep interior core of our being where we take our stand toward God, or away from God (toward self!), toward truth or falsity. Our actions are the living, revelatory signs of whether or not we are loving as Christ loved—as we were charged to do.

The term "conscience" appears only once in the Old Testa-ment (Wis 17:11), not at all in the gospels (although Jesus calls the people to greater response to interior dispositions, rather than to law), but some thirty times in the New Testament letters, especially in St. Paul.[9] In the latter instances the context is one in which persons are charged to adopt a basic life vision that would then govern and be reflected in their actions—consistent with developing a Christian moral character.

## THE AUTHORITY OF PERSONAL CONSCIENCE

Recognizing the importance of persons assuming responsi-bility for their own lives and actions as an expression of human dignity and freedom, the Catechism says that "they must never be constrained to act against their consciences, nor impeded from acting in keeping with their consciences, especially in religious matters"(§ 1783).[10]

For many Catholics this authority of personal conscience has a new ring to it. It wasn't highly stressed, if even mentioned, in for-mal religious training at the elementary or even secondary school levels. The church's teaching on the freedom and authority of conscience is not new, however. For example, the Fourth Lateran Council (AD 1215) stated that "he who acts against his conscience loses his soul." Thomas Aquinas wrote that "anyone upon whom the ecclesiastical authority, in ignorance of true facts, imposes a demand that offends against his clear conscience should perish in excommunication rather than violate his conscience."[11]

Unfortunately, there is a tendency in the face of this recovered teaching on personal conscience's authority for some persons, especially the theologically unsophisticated, the minimally catechized, or the ethically dishonest to think that authoritative teachings of the church are simply other opinions to be considered. In view of this, and without denying the freedom and authority of personal conscience, the Catechism offers some legitimate cautions.

> We must always obey the certain judgment of conscience. Should we act deliberately against it, we would condemn ourselves. Yet our moral conscience may remain in ignorance and so could bring incorrect judgments to bear on acts proposed or already committed (§ 1790).

> People often bear personal responsibility for this ignorance, as "when someone shows scant concern for seeking the true and good and when conscience is gradually blinded from the habit of sin."[12] In such cases, the person is guilty of the evil he or she commits (§ 1791).

> Ignorance of Christ and the gospel, the bad example of others, slavery to the passions, *the claim to a misunderstood autonomy of conscience, rejection of the church's authority and teaching* (emphasis added), and lack of conversion and love can be the beginning of deviations from right judgment in moral conduct (§ 1792).[13]

## THE FORMATION OF CONSCIENCE

This brings us, finally (!), to the original and central purpose of this essay: the formation of conscience. In both the traditional and the contemporary treatment of conscience the *fact* of a personal conscience is a given, whether one calls it *synderesis* (the Catechism) or Conscience/1. This first level of conscience simply acknowledges that every person is born with an innate desire to do good and avoid evil, a basic sense of responsibility that characterizes the human person.

The nature of what is the "good" and the "evil" is the focus of Conscience/2 ("moral science" in the manuals; acknowledged but unnamed in the Catechism). According to the Catechism, the principles of morality perceived at level one are, at level two, applied "in the given circumstances by practical discernment between principles and values" (§ 1780). It is at this second level of conscience that conscience formation takes place.

The Catechism speaks of conscience formation in three brief paragraphs. We will look at each one separately.

> Conscience must be informed and moral judgment enlightened. A well-formed conscience is upright and true. It formulates its judgment in accordance with reason, in keeping with the true good willed by the creator's wisdom. The formation of conscience is essential to human beings, who are subject to many negative influences and tempted by sin to prefer their own judgment and to reject authoritative teachings (§ 1783).

Here the Catechism acknowledges that the innate moral sense (*synderesis*) must be informed and educated[14] in order to develop in the individual a conscience that is "upright and true."[15] This formation (the French text uses *L'education*) of conscience according to the true order established by the creator is rooted primarily in human reason and is essential for authentic human moral development. Without it, the negative influences of this world, the reality of selfish self-interest, and the propensity to reject authoritative teachings might well fill in the void. The Catechism does not elaborate on particulars here, but will do so to a degree in the treatment of the decalogue, where each commandment is addressed according to potential infringements.

The Catechism continues:

> The formation of conscience is a lifelong task. From the earliest years, this formation awakens the child to an understanding and acceptance of the inner law recognized by the moral conscience. Prudent education teaches virtue and prevents or

corrects fear, selfishness, pride, feelings of guilt and the movements of complacency, born of weakness and human failings.
The formation of conscience guarantees freedom and engenders peace of heart (§ 1784).

Conscience is not formed once and for all. It is subject to ongoing formation and reformation as we come to more clearly and
fully understand the "inner law recognized" by Conscience/1 (*synderesis*). This ongoing formation calls for "prudent education"—
a task laid at the feet of all who are presumed to be value commu-
nicators, bishops, yes, but first parents, family, and society that are
in place to make the first indelible impact on children.

The final sentence is especially striking, I believe: "The formation of conscience guarantees freedom and engenders peace
of heart." The assumption here is that we are only and always talking about formation of a true or right conscience. That being the
case, if such has been the honest goal of the individual, then he or
she, judging and acting honestly, is truly free or liberated from
doubt or guilt. In another sense, the person whose conscience has
been well formed is able to make his or her own decisions and, in
so doing, is liberated from the operation of the superego and
takes ownership of his or her decisions.

The final paragraph on formation of conscience calls us to
let the word of God be our guide and faith and prayer be our en-
abler. The prompting of the Holy Spirit helping us to interpret
the realities of experience, the advice of others on the journey,
and the authoritative teaching of the church each contributes to
this enterprise.

> In the formation of conscience God's word is a light to our path;
> we are to assimilate the word in faith and prayer and so put it
> into practice. We should examine our consciences in the light
> of the Lord's cross, helped by the gifts of the Holy Spirit, aided
> by the witness or advice of others and guided by the church's
> authoritative teaching (§ 1785).

No detailed list of instructions for the right and proper formation of moral conscience is attempted by the Catechism. We
are encouraged to stay close to the word of God and the authoritative teachings of the church in anticipation of and subsequent

evaluation of our moral decisions. In closing this section on conscience, the Catechism calls attention to reasons why malformation of conscience, and, therefore, poor moral decisions, take place.

> Ignorance of Christ and his gospel, the bad example of others, slavery to the passions, the claim to a misunderstood autonomy of conscience, rejection of the church's authority and teaching, and lack of conversion and love can be the beginning of deviations from right judgment in moral conduct (§ 1792).

In reviewing what the Catechism has to say about the formation of conscience I have sought to discern something of the underlying moral vision and theological methodology in Book Three (Life in Christ) because formation or education tends toward some goal. The stated goal of the Catechism is to provide a resource for those whose task it is to assist believers in living the gospel of Jesus Christ: To love as Christ loved. Toward that end the Catechism offers to the universal church guidelines that are consistent with the traditional, authoritative teachings of the magisterium.

# CATECHESIS FOR JUSTICE AND PEACE IN THE CATECHISM

# James L. Nash

The subject of catechesis for justice and peace in the *Catechism of the Catholic Church* raises two questions that in my judgment are fundamental and interrelated. First, what does the struggle for social justice have to do with faith in Jesus Christ? This question is directed, *ad intra*, to the church's own self-understanding. Is Roman Catholic social teaching an extraneous modern development tacked on to the church's teaching in a belated attempt to appear "relevant" to modern secular people? Or is action on behalf of justice and peace an integral part of living the gospel?

The second question I want to focus on is related to the church, *ad extra*, and concerns its mission to the world. What difference, if any, does Christian faith make in the worldly struggle for justice and peace? At the Second Vatican Council, there was a call for dialogue between the church and the world;[1] but for a dialogue to take place there must be two parties, each of whom has something to say. There are many people without religious faith who are working very hard and very effectively to build a more just and peaceful world. Does the Catechism show that the church has something to say to them that could be worth listening to?

A dialogue also requires that both parties listen to one another. Does the new Catechism offer evidence that the church has learned something about justice and peace from the world? In many ways the dialogue partners I have in mind here are represented by the undergraduate students I have taught at The Catholic University of America over the past several years. From them I have learned that a necessary condition for the reception of the church's mission to the world is clear evidence that the church itself is just and is capable of listening to and learning from the action of the Spirit in the world.

We have learned from some of the other papers of this symposium that those responsible for the *Catechism of the Catholic Church* are well aware that the document must be received by the local church, and adapted to the concrete cultural conditions of the community. In what follows I attempt to do this, to show, in other words, some of the moves I would make in using the teachings of the Catechism in my undergraduate religion classes. The students of Catholic University are typical in many ways of young adults in our country who have a basic Catholic background. Many of them are alienated from the institutional church, and those who are not frequently have a very privatized understanding of their faith, and are by no means convinced that the church has anything meaningful to say to them about the urgent moral and political problems of our day. The two questions that I am asking address these related problems.

I begin to answer the first question, whether and how the church has learned from the Spirit of God in the world, by a brief comparison of the new Catechism with the older Roman Catechism that grew out of the Council of Trent. My approach is open to the criticism that I exaggerate the changes and under-report the continuities between the two documents. However, given the nature of my question and the audience I have in mind I think this is a legitimate strategy.

Moreover, in the field of the church's moral teaching on justice and peace, there has been a considerable amount of development and refinement since the time of the Council of Trent. Perhaps nowhere has the church been called upon to adapt itself more than in the areas of justice and peace, as the social and cultural changes that have occurred in the past four centuries are enormous. Rather than fearing that changes or developments in the church's moral teachings might undermine its teaching authority, I believe quite the reverse is true. Good teachers increase their authority and effectiveness by changing their lesson plans in the light of students' questions and concerns.

Throughout my examination I will be concentrating on the way the new Catechism handles two basic themes that are especially relevant in answering my two questions: 1) the christological basis of the moral life; 2) the organic relationship between personal sin and structural evil.

## COMPARING THE *CCC* AND THE TRIDENTINE CATECHISM ON THE MORAL LIFE

The only other catechism intended for the universal church was issued over four hundred years ago in the wake of the Council of Trent. This fact alone invites us to compare the *Catechism of the Catholic Church* with the older Tridentine document. The fact that the new Catechism has adopted the same four-part structure as the old has provoked serious and legitimate criticism by many commentators, which I need not repeat here. However, this decision to use the "old wineskins" of the Council of Trent has the advantage of aiding the comparison of the two texts.

The location of the moral teaching in the third book in both catechisms is significant: it expresses an essential point of continuity between the documents and it also grounds one of my major themes. The Christian moral life is not the first moment in the life of faith; rather, it is a response to God's revelation of love for us. Our moral life is our ability to respond, or our "response-ability" to God's gracious love, revealed in Jesus Christ. I believe that this is both a metaphysical and a psychological truth. Unless we first experience love, by God and neighbor, we will be unable to respond.

At the same time, the four-part structure does raise the problem of whether or to what extent the moral teaching is integrated into the material on creeds, sacraments, and prayer. The text of the *CCC* does contain many cross-references, placed in the margins, which help the reader to see the connections between various aspects of doctrine; however there are limits that result from the structure of the Catechism, despite its frequent references to the "organic unity" of the faith.

The opposite of organic is sterile, and sterility is what results when the church's moral teachings are presented in isolation from the "first moment" of God's revelation of love for us, and the "third moment" of God's forgiveness for our moral lapses. Whether it is the course syllabus or the need to compensate for inadequate catechesis that compels me to specialize in one dimension of church teaching, I find it critical to emphasize repeatedly to my students that the church's moral doctrine is intrinsically connected to Jesus' disclosure of God's love for all human beings. Jesus' moral message is demanding, and if it is severed from the experience of God's mysterious love for us, there will be an almost irresistible temptation either to reject the challenge as unrealistic, or to water it down with the comforts of pragmatic and utilitarian considerations.

As indicated above, both documents address the Christian moral life in Book Three. In the Tridentine document this book is entitled simply "The Ten Commandments," and after a brief introductory section on the importance of obeying these commandments, the rest of the book concentrates on explaining their import for the Christian life.

It is significant that Book Three in the new Catechism is entitled "Life in Christ." In addition, the more christological understanding of moral life is underscored by the inclusion of an entire section that precedes the discussion of the ten commandments and that is devoted to a theological account of human action and morality. The starting point for this section is the dignity of the human person as the image of God, rooted in our creation by God and redemption in Christ. A central theme of this discussion, and of John Paul II's pontificate, is taken from *Gaudium et Spes:* "Christ, 'by revealing the mystery of the Father and his love . . . fully discloses what it is to be human and manifests the nobility of our calling'" (§ 1071; *GS* 22).[2] While the new Catechism does affirm the traditional authority of the magisterium to interpret the specific demands of the natural law (§ 2036), more emphasis is given to the christological basis for the church's claims of authority about the moral life, especially when compared to the *Roman Catechism.* I shall return to this theme below.

The social dimension of the human person, another important theme of Vatican II, is emphasized in a second chapter, "The Human Community." Finally, in order to place the discussion of the obligations of the ten commandments in the proper theological perspective, there is a chapter on "Law and Grace."

## JUSTICE AND THE SEVENTH COMMANDMENT

In order to understand some of the specific consequences of this more theological approach to the themes of justice and peace, it is necessary to examine their treatment under the seventh and fifth commandments, respectively. The discussion of the seventh commandment in the Catechism of the Council of Trent is based primarily on the defense of private property, and includes a tax-onomy of the various forms of theft, a section on the duty of resti-tution, and a concluding section on the duty of almsgiving to the poor.

When we look at the new Catechism's treatment of the in-junction against theft, there are five specific themes that reveal the results of new theological reflection. Again, it is creation and incarnation-redemption that appear to be primary sources here, although in my judgment one can also detect the contributions of liberation theology in the treatment of several of these topics.

First, the article begins with the principle of the universal des-tiny of created goods. God created the earth and its resources for the entire human race. Thus we can locate the boundaries as well as the *raison d'être* of the right to private property within this broad-er theological framework. "The *universal purpose of goods* remains fundamental, even if the promotion of the common good requires respect for private property . . ." (§ 2403). Consequently, this com-mandment not only forbids the unjust taking of our neighbor's goods, but more positively it also requires that owners of the means of production must take care that their stewardship will profit the greatest number of people. In addition, political authorities have the right and duty to regulate the right to private property for the sake of the common good. The right to private property is not absolute.

Respect for the integrity of creation also grounds our treat-ment of animals, plants, and inanimate beings. The *Catechism of the Catholic Church* is one of the first catechetical documents to emerge from Rome that expresses this new moral imperative. The human dominion over the created world, referred to in Genesis, is not absolute (§ 2415). There is need for a "religious respect for creation's integrity." It is thought-provoking that this ecological con-cern is placed in the context of the commandment against theft. In one sense it is true that by exploiting excessively the earth's re-sources we are stealing from future generations as well as those currently living on the planet who must live with the consequences of foul air and water—even if they do not share in the benefits.

Finally, three more interrelated themes in this section on the seventh commandment deserve to be highlighted as results of the church's social teaching: the "love of preference" for the poor, the critique of the structures of modern global capitalism, and a very strong appeal for international justice. They indicate sensitivity to issues raised by liberation theology.

Those who are oppressed by poverty "are the object of a love of preference on the part of the church" (§ 2448). It is true that the Catechism's language here is somewhat muted, and it avoids the phrase "preferential option for the poor." On the other hand, the "love of preference" for the poor is clearly one fruit of grounding moral reflection more deeply in the life of Jesus and our redemption in Christ—nothing like it can be found in the *Roman Catechism.* It is also related to changes in the political and economic context during the past four hundred years.

Previous understandings of the common good entailed the view that special preference be shown to *no* particular group within society; moreover, fundamental socio-economic inequalities were presupposed to be "natural." The contradictions of the modern social situation have led to the recognition that the common good is now best served by an explicit preference for the poor. In the post-Tridentine period, there has been an enormous increase in the demand for basic equality; and while there has been some growth in the recognition of political equality, there is simultaneously an acute awareness of huge economic inequalities, both within nations and between the nations of the northern and the southern regions. The recognition that basic socio-economic inequalities are not entirely "natural" but rather socially determined greatly increases the moral urgency of dealing with poverty. There is then a social as well as a theological logic to the preferential option for the poor.

Almsgiving is thus now not merely enjoined as a duty of charity, but St. John Chrysostom is quoted as saying "not to enable the poor to share in our goods is to steal from them and deprive them of life" (§ 2446). Giving to the poor is first a matter of justice, not charity.

Perhaps the strongest language in the entire third book on the Christian life can be found under the heading "Justice and Solidarity Among Nations" (§§ 2437ff). Here we read, "On the international level, the inequality of resources and economic means is such that it creates a veritable abyss among nations." One of the motives behind the creation of the Catechism is the concern to promote worldwide Christian unity; the enormous gap between rich and poor countries is a fundamental "sign of the times" that threatens the unity of the church every bit as much as the unity of the planet.[3] In the current situation, to speak of a moral "abyss" (Fr. *fossè*), as the Catechism does (§ 2437), is appropriate, in my judgment. The enormous gap between the developed and undeveloped nations is actually widening. The Catechism discusses the two responses to this crisis that are now both essential parts of Roman Catholic social teaching. There is first of all the need for direct aid (§ 2440). This is similar to the traditional Christian response of almsgiving to the poor.

In addition, the Catechism recognizes that acts of charity by individuals or nations are insufficient to achieve global justice: the problem is also structural. International economic and financial institutions must be reformed. International free trade, which the United States claims to favor, makes possible the domination of the weak by the economically powerful. The debt crisis, the low price paid for raw materials, and the high price paid for industrial goods are concrete examples of how an uncritical dedication to the ideology of free trade justifies the continuing impoverishment of the poorer nations. This is related to the fundamental principle that the goods of creation and economic activity must first of all serve the needs of the human person, and "there are many human needs which find no place in the market" (§ 2425).

The powerful new understanding of the "organic" connection between unjust structures and the traditional Christian focus on personal sin is revealed in paragraph 1887:

> The inversion of means and ends, which assigns the value of an ultimate end to what is only a means for attaining it or regards persons as mere means for achieving other ends, engenders unjust structures. These in turn make Christian conduct, in keeping with the commandments of the divine law-giver, difficult—even impossible—in practice.

To say that unjust structures can make Christian conduct impossible is a very strong critique that echoes the position of many liberation theologians. The new Catechism is also well aware that just as sinful structures cause personal sin, personal inner conversion is a necessary pre-condition for the change of these structures (§ 1888); this points to the virtue of social justice, which is perhaps the most critical concept of Roman Catholic social teaching.

A proper understanding of social justice helps to illustrate the connectedness between the personal and the structural, which may be distinctive of Roman Catholic social teaching. Pius XI, who introduced the concept, was concerned in part about the moral dilemma faced by a just Catholic employer who, because of the low market value of his employees' labor, was unable to pay them a living wage without going out of business. It seemed unjust, and ultimately self-defeating, to require the employer to go bankrupt in order to pay a living wage; yet it also would be a serious injustice if the obligation were completely dispensed.

Pius XI's response was to hold that while the employer need not pay the just wage immediately, he or she was obligated to try to reform the structural injustice that prevented the payment of decent wages. This obligation was described as falling under social justice. In concrete terms this meant working to pass reasonable minimum wage laws, so that the competition would be obliged to pay its workers fairly.

Thus social justice is not some vaguely left-wing abstract state of affairs which one demands that *others* bring about; it is the personal obligation an individual has to change the structures that make sinful behavior inevitable in the modern context. Social justice is a virtue that expresses the organic connectedness of personal and structural sin and reform.

While the Catechism does speak about social justice in its discussion of the seventh commandment, it does not clearly bring out its personal dimension as a virtue (§ 2426) nor does it discuss social justice in the section devoted to the virtues (§§ 1804ff).[4] Instead, there is an article devoted to social justice in the chapter on the human community (§§ 1928ff). Here the personal, virtuous dimension of social justice is not developed as clearly as it could be; instead, it tends to be treated more as an abstract state of affairs. Given the Catechism's emphasis on both the structural and personal aspects of sin and reform, I believe its failure to develop social justice as the virtue that connects these two dimensions is a regrettable oversight.

At any rate, it can be seen that the three themes of the preference for the poor, international justice, and structural change are all interrelated. The Catechism teaches us that the genuine gospel value of the "love of preference for the poor" in the modern context requires a dedication to changing the unjust national and international trade and financial structures that are responsible for much of the growing impoverishment of the world's peoples.

## CATECHESIS FOR PEACE AND
## THE FIFTH COMMANDMENT

I have thus far said little about the theme of "catechesis for peace," but according to the Catechism, the issue of international justice is intrinsically connected to global peace in at least two ways. First, the international arms race absorbs material resources that could be used to foster economic development (§ 2438).[5] Second, genuine peace among nations is impossible so long as the enormous gap in wealth continues to grow.

Time does not permit a detailed comparison of the treatment of the fifth commandment (against murder) in the *Roman Catechism* and in the *Catechism of the Catholic Church*. However, additional evidence for what I have referred to as the christological grounding of morality in the new Catechism can be found in the inclusion of a quotation from Matthew's gospel, placed directly below the Old Testament commandment, thus forming a point of departure for the following article. The quotation is from the sermon on the mount, in which Jesus radicalizes the teaching of the old law against murder: "But I say to you that if you are angry with a brother or sister, you will be liable to judgment" (§ 2258).

In the *Catechism of the Council of Trent*, after a few paragraphs on the importance of the Old Testament commandment, there are several straightforward sections on the exceptions to the rule: the killing of animals, the execution of criminals, killing in a just war, by accident, and self-defense. In the *Roman Catechism* war appears to be treated as an inevitable part of human life, there is no provision for those who due to conscience might refuse military service, and there is even reference to the "instances of carnage executed by the special command of God."[6] The discussion of peace—the positive part of the commandment—is directed primarily to the right ordering of individual relationships. Although there is a beautiful section on the necessity of charity for the cultivation of peace, it is disappointing that there is no discussion of the connection between justice and peace, nor anything on the relationship between structural injustice and violence.

The new Catechism's approach differs in both style and substance from the *Roman Catechism.* The *Catechism of the Catholic Church* begins its discussion of war by urging everyone to pray that God may free us from "the ancient bondage of war." In addition, following the teaching of Vatican II, it directs public authorities to allow for conscientious objectors to military service. At the same time, "the right of legitimate self-defense cannot be denied to governments" so long as there is no competent international authority with the necessary powers. However, the document has a "preferential option" for peace, which can be seen inasmuch as the whole discussion of the legitimacy of national self-defense falls under the main heading "Safeguarding Peace" and the sub-heading "Avoiding War" (§§ 2302, 2307).

What is distinctive about the discussion of peace in the new Catechism is the attempt to link the personal dimension of peacemaking with its structural or political aspects. Anger, hatred, the refusal to forgive a neighbor or to love an enemy are obviously inimical to peace. Neither personal nor international peace is the mere absence of war, nor is peace achieved by assuring the balance of opposing powers. Genuine peace is a positive reality that cannot be obtained without respect for the dignity of individual persons and nations. "Injustice, excessive inequality in the economic or social order, envy, mistrust and pride raging among peoples and nations continue to threaten peace and cause wars (§ 2317). Perhaps the attempted synthesis is best summed up by a line that is based on a section in *Gaudium et Spes:* "Peace is the work of justice and the effect of charity" (§ 2304).[7]

## POSITIVE DEVELOPMENTS IN MORAL THEOLOGY

This brief exposition of the *Catechism of the Catholic Church* has highlighted the developments that have taken place in the theological and moral teachings of the church since the Council of Trent. These developments reflect the profound historical changes that have occurred in the last four hundred years in the socio-

economic field as well as in the nature of modern warfare. I believe there is plenty of evidence to answer affirmatively the question asked at the beginning—whether or not the church is capable
of learning from the action of the Spirit in the world. Theologically,
at the deepest level the shift can be seen in a more christological
grounding of the Christian moral life. This christological shift is
expressed in such broad themes as the fundamental dignity of the
human person, the "love of preference for the poor," and a height-
ened sense that war is avoidable and that every Christian needs to
work actively for peace and justice on the personal and political
level.

A second development, equally fundamental, which lies more
properly in the moral domain, is the recognition that a full response
to the gospel must involve responsibility for the structural dimension of social, political, and economic life. This is related to the insistent assertion in *Gaudium et Spes* that the human person is by
nature a social being. But it is also related to the modern world's
having "come of age"; people today are aware that it is we ourselves who construct our social and economic reality.

In what follows I hope to draw on these two fundamental moral
and theological developments in order to push further the critical
questions posed at the beginning of the essay—namely, has the
church learned from the world, and can the world learn something
from the church? My basic thesis in this section is that the positive
fruits of the new Catechism's attention to christology and to the
structural dimension of sin are inconsistent with its rather defensive ecclesiology. I believe that what is missing from the Catechism
is a critique of church praxis and structure, for if one is to do a
credible presentation of the church teaching on justice and peace,
a candid acknowledgment of its own shortcomings and failures is
a pre-requisite.

## THE MORAL LIFE AND THE PRAXIS OF THE CHURCH

First, with respect to praxis, there are plenty of documents
coming from Rome and from the National Conference of Catholic Bishops that affirm the unity of justice and faith in Jesus Christ.
One of the strongest statements to emerge in recent years, lamentably not cited in the Catechism, is from the 1971 Synod of Bish-

ops document "Justice in the World," where one reads that "Action on behalf of justice and participation in the transformation of the world fully appear to us as a constitutive dimension of the preaching of the gospel."[8]

In my teaching the first basic problem is empirical. For the majority of students and believers who have grown up in the church, there is little knowledge or even awareness of the existence of Roman Catholic social teaching. The title of a recent work, *Our Best Kept Secret—Roman Catholic Social Teaching,* describes the situation. On the one hand it is exciting to see the eyes of students light up when they discover that the church has been reflecting on these important issues for over a century; but on the other hand this is profoundly disturbing given that so many of them come from relatively devout Roman Catholic backgrounds.

There are no doubt many causes for this phenomenon. One of the most powerful is connected to the *ad extra* issues that I will take up below, that is, the influence of modern culture and the liberal understanding of religion as an utterly individualistic privatized reality. For many of my students the "separation of church and state" means that the church has no right to say anything whatsoever about the political or economic order.

However, if action on behalf of justice is a constitutive dimension of preaching the gospel, these are all powerful reasons for emphasizing the centrality of the church's social justice tradition, and criticizing past and present failures forcefully. One is also entitled to ask what role the concern for justice plays in the typical Sunday homily, in the liturgy of the word and in the normal sacramental life of the church. Does action on behalf of justice appear rather to be an optional piece of "do-goodism," something which is peripheral to that which is central: the consoling, personal, "feel-good" religion of the suburbs? It appears as though, despite many fine documents, the church's social justice tradition is all too often not lived as an integral part of the life of faith. This raises anew the problematic decision of using the four-part Tridentine structure, which tends to separate morality from other aspects of doctrine.

This problem is primarily a practical problem, but it is also rooted in a certain kind of theology. For some members of the church there is an actual conflict between social justice and the handing on of the faith. Michael J. Wrenn has recently written a little book entitled *Catechisms and Controversies,* in which he writes, "The very people charged with the task of finding better and more effective ways of handing on the faith unilaterally decide that what is important is not handing on the faith at all, but rather the struggle for social justice. . . ."[9] According to Wrenn this represents a shift in catechesis from God to man, from proclaiming the good news of salvation in Jesus Christ to espousing a purely human kind of effort featuring a struggling humanity trying to save itself by political means from oppression and injustice.

I believe that a careful reading of the documents of Vatican II and the *Catechism of the Catholic Church* reveals how wrong-headed this theological approach is. But Wrenn's critique also reveals a theological and practical problem afflicting the church that is not clearly addressed by the Catechism. His critique can also serve as a helpful challenge to those of us who do social ethics, because it presupposes that the struggle for social justice is a purely secular and human phenomenon, untouched by grace or faith. This presupposition raises again the two questions with which I began: 1) Is not God's Spirit at work in the world in such a way that the church can come to apprehend more deeply the meaning of Christ's salvific love by attending to the "secular" struggle for justice and peace? 2) Does explicit faith in Jesus Christ affect concretely the way believers do justice and peace, so that it is different in some ways from the struggle of those without this faith commitment?[10]

## INSTITUTIONAL AND STRUCTURAL SIN IN THE CHURCH AND ITS DENIAL

I have already given some of the reasons why I believe the first question can be answered affirmatively. There is however still something crucial that is missing from this picture of what and how the church learns from the world, something that cannot clearly be found in any conciliar document, and that is also lamentably absent from the Catechism. Earlier in this essay I noted that one critical development in the church's understanding of the world is the notion of the structural dimension of evil or sin. While there are several references to the sinfulness of the *members* of the church in this text (§§ 817–819),[11] there is little recognition (§ 825)[12] that the church itself may suffer from structural evil or distortions.[13] How is the recognition that the church is made up of sinners to be reconciled with the affirmation that the church as an "entity" is holy? Can one speak of the "church of sinners" without also speaking of the sinful church? The failure of the Catechism to recognize structural evil within the church is particularly anomalous, given the power with which it condemns sinful social structures in the world.

In affirming the right to religious freedom, for example, the Catechism offers no historical background about the church's own ambiguous relationship to this right (§§ 2104ff). The Catechism thus squanders the opportunity to show that the church is confident and humble enough to affirm serenely that on this point it has learned something concrete and essential about justice and peace from the world.

Has the church's historical failure to recognize fully the right to religious freedom truly been only a case of individual Christians who occasionally had a distorted understanding of the demands of the gospel and justice? Was not the distortion here more systematic and institutional? Of course the understanding of the moral demands of the gospel is bound to be historically conditioned. Therefore what is problematic is not the denial of the gospel involved in the historical failure fully to respect the value of religious freedom, or other historical examples of the church's sinfulness. In my judgment what is deeply troubling and of urgent importance today is the *denial of this denial.*

This is where the issue of the church's own justice is intrinsically connected to the credibility of its mission to preach the gospel of justice and peace to the world. Many of my students are unwilling to listen to the church's message of justice and peace because they are convinced that there are structural injustices built into the church today, particularly with respect to the treatment of women, but also having to do with the handling of priests guilty of sexual abuse, with financial accountability, and with the treatment of minority groups.

That the church has sometimes been guilty of injustice is one thing, but that this should be denied or covered up is much more disturbing. This is related to the problem identified earlier about identifying the church as a whole too closely with the "already" of realized eschatology. One of the ways justice and peace are connected is that many people are simply not prepared to be at peace with the church until the record is straight on the church's own internal witness to justice. The gospel itself tells us that the critical first step in this process is to name and own up to the failings. If the church truly believes in dialogue with the world, that it can learn something from this dialogue, that structural evil is a reality in the world, and that the church is a church of sinners, why is it so difficult to acknowledge that there may have been and may still be structural evil within the church itself?

Perhaps one clue can be found in the Catechism's affirmations that the Roman church is both apostolic (§ 811) and Petrine (§ 838). As Karl Barth pointed out in his *Church Dogmatics,* it is thought-provoking that although the four evangelists knew at the time they were writing their gospels that Judas betrayed Jesus, they all insist in their writings that Judas was *one of the twelve.* It might have been tempting, as one was writing the history of Jesus' movement, to deduce that because of his betrayal of Jesus, Judas could not, in retrospect, have been a genuine apostle. Yet this is a move that none of the gospel writers make: they all insist that Judas was one of the twelve. The conclusion seems inescapable: the betrayal of Jesus is something that belongs to the highest and most intimate level of the church's apostolic ministry. At the same time this betrayal in no way threatens to destroy the genuine apostolic authority of the church. But if this is so, then why is there a denial of the denial?

The church is also Petrine. St. Peter was perhaps most human, and most lovable, when he insisted that he would never deny Jesus (Mt 26:35). This is the same Peter who, in rejecting Jesus' prophecy of his own crucifixion, is also criticized by Jesus for thinking as men think, rather than as God thinks (Mt 16:23). Could it be that the *Catechism of the Catholic Church* also is following in this all-too-human tradition of St. Peter by continuing to deny the church's occasional structural denial of Jesus, perhaps also out of fear of what men will think, rather than trusting in the power of God to forgive any sin that is confessed? If the Roman Catholic Church is both the body of Christ as well as Petrine, is there still a typically Petrine refusal to accept the need for the church's crucifixion?

In any event, the recognition of the right to religious freedom is, in my judgment, one historical piece of evidence that the church can learn something about the demands of justice and peace from the world. The argument for the frank recognition that the church of sinners is also a sinful church is that the admission would help to strengthen the church-world dialogue, further justice and peace within the church, and better enable the church to perform its mission of service to the world.

## THE ECLIPSE OF RELIGIOUS ETHICS IN SOCIETY

In the final part of this essay I would like to turn my attention to the *ad extra* dimension of the church–world dialogue. It is precisely because I believe that the church, truly inspired by the Holy Spirit, has a distinctive contribution to make to the world in the area of peace and justice, a contribution that is obscured by the denial of the denial, that I believe it is crucial for the Catholic Church to confess its own sinfulness.

One can by no means assume that there is an affirmative answer to the question of whether or not the church has something distinctive and substantive to offer the world on the issues of justice and peace. There are first of all a growing number of advocates for "neutral" politics who believe that disputed beliefs about human goods should play no or at most a marginal role in public political discourse; some of these writers explicitly wish to exclude religious beliefs from public conversation.[14]

There are a number of possible responses to this line of argument. For example, it is possible for the church to speak of the natural moral law that is founded on reason and therefore open to all. But there is today widespread confusion and debate, both inside and outside the church, about the content and even the rational validity of the natural law. This is part of the reason why, as I have argued, the Catechism bases much of its authority in the moral area on christological grounds—without disowning the natural law tradition.

Jeffrey Stout is one of the few moral philosophers writing today who takes religious ethics seriously. In his book *Ethics After Babel*[15] he takes for granted that theology has lost its public voice, and laments the eclipse of religious ethics in our society. Stout is critical of the effort by theologians to adopt the philosophical methods and presuppositions of other disciplines, as "there is no more certain way for theology to lose its voice than to imitate that of another."[16] Secular intellectuals do not need to be told by theologians that Genesis is mythical, that nobody knows much about the historical Jesus, or that it is morally imperative to side with the oppressed. The eclipse of religious ethics in our time may be due simply to the fact "that academic theologians are increasingly giving the impression of saying nothing atheists don't already know."[17]

Stout holds that in the public arena today a hearing for theological ideas can no longer be taken for granted, but must be won, if they are to get a hearing at all. For the dialogue to take place theology must have something distinctive, something recognizably theological, to say. It must make clear what difference theology makes and how an educated person could reasonably believe its disputed and distinctive claims.[18]

I can here respond only briefly to the challenge posed to theology by Jeffrey Stout. I will attempt to show how using the theological treatment of justice and peace in the Catechism as a basis, one can make a distinctive contribution to public life and discourse. My thoughts can be grouped around two different poles. First, using the Catechism's vision of the nature of structural and personal sin, a positive response can be framed to the "crisis of meaning" that is characteristic of today's political and social life.[19] Secondly I will offer some christological observations on the relationship between justice and peace.

Many people feel alienated from the "boxes" of both left and right wing secular ideologies; they believe that the traditional ideological differences between the political parties are increasingly meaningless. A second problem is that people feel "disconnected" from society and politics; there is a widespread dissatisfaction with the excessive individualism and materialism of rights-based interest-group liberalism. Third, there is a sense of hopelessness and helplessness: many people have come to feel personally powerless in the face of the enormous systematic problems we face.

I believe that Christian theology can address these related problems through reflection on the meaning of sin, redemption-eschatology, and the church; however I will here limit myself to a single point. One way of understanding the bankruptcy of left and right wing secular ideologies is to argue that each suffers from a partial notion of where to locate evil and human sinfulness. The

Christian vision of the mystery of sin as expressed in the Catechism holds that sin is always essentially a personal choice, and yet
at the same time sin is something that is always already present to
us even before it is chosen. And the sin that is already always out
there conditions the sin that is freely chosen.

I have highlighted how the *Catechism of the Catholic Church* differs from the *Roman Catechism* in attacking the sin that is present
in the structures of the world as well as in the human heart. The
Catechism speaks often of the "organic unity of the faith." I believe it is important for Christian theology to criticize, or even to
rule out, excessive adherence to either left or right wing ideologies,
and to affirm the organic unity of personal and structural evil, as
well as the need for both personal and structural reform.

What is distinctive of right wing ideologies is the refusal to take
seriously structural sin and the need for structural reform. Such
an approach prefers to speak about peace and justice issues like
abortion and euthanasia because they seem to be based on personally sinful choices—and they are. Yet the choice to abort is not un-
related to enormous structural evil in our society having to do
with the status of women and children, sexuality and health care.
A full treatment of this issue cannot neglect structural injustices.

The problems of global hunger and modern warfare are rooted in evils that seem more structural than personal, and so left wing
ideologies are more comfortable in taking up these issues. But the
failure of systems is the result of many personal failures of individuals. With respect to capital punishment, the right is focused on
the sin of the convict, the left on the sin of the system that has condemned him or her.

Yet, if one is convinced that sin is both personal and by analogy structural, why is it necessary to choose between the left and
the right? Why is it not possible to insist on the highest standards
of both personal responsibility and structural reform? The positive expression of this critique of secular ideologies can be seen in
the consistent ethic of life espoused by Cardinal  Bernardin, in
which all the peace and justice issues are connected. It is regrettable that the Catechism does not make this explicit connection,
but it does strongly affirm the organic relationship between structural and personal sin in a way that challenges and may even help
to unite the artificial distinctions of both the left and right, ide-

ologies that unfortunately all too often divide the church as well as the world.

## THE CHURCH'S DISTINCTIVE WITNESS TO JUSTICE AND PEACE

In addition to the personal and structural understanding of human sin, I have highlighted the Catechism's christological grounding of the moral life. The final question I want to pose is whether there is here a distinctive and substantive contribution that the church can make to the world's search for justice and peace.

The Catechism lays the groundwork for a positive answer, but it unfortunately fails to highlight the distinctively Christian witness of creative, active non-violence. In order to address this question of the church's distinctive witness to justice and peace it is obviously necessary to define what is meant by these frequently used words. The classical and Thomistic definition of justice used in the Catechism (§ 1807) is that it is a virtue which leads a person to give what is due to God and neighbor. To say that justice is a virtue means that it is an inner disposition, a personal strength, which is also objective inasmuch as, unlike affective virtues, it regards the other, and connotes equality. Too often in the modern world when we speak of the demands of justice or social justice, we tend to assume that it is an abstract state of affairs that some other person or institution must somehow bring about; or that justice entails only the claiming of my rights, without regard to my responsibilities. As I noted previously, the concept of social justice expresses the connection between personal and structural dimensions of the virtue, between rights and responsibilities.

The dual nature of the word "peace" is no doubt clearer to us. We speak of the need for world peace and at the same time we "pass the peace" to those standing near to us in the liturgy. The Catechism quotes St. Augustine who spoke of peace as the "tranquility of order" (§ 2304), and one can see that this is no less true of a society than it is of what is going on inside each person who makes up a society.

When the Catechism links peace and justice by affirming that injustice threatens peace and causes wars, one needs to bear in mind the organic interplay between the personal and the structural aspects of both justice and peace. It is no doubt empirically true that peace and justice are positively correlated. Moreover, just as injustice can lead to war, war itself fosters more injustice.

However, I also believe that in some sense there is a tension between justice and peace, just as there is a connection and yet a tension between justice and love. This tension points to the necessity of a christological understanding of both justice and peace—something that is pointed to, albeit implicitly, in the Catechism's traditional appeal for love and forgiveness as the ultimate answer to war and injustice (§§ 2317, 2262).

Most of the violent conflicts between people as well as between nations are rooted in the demand for justice, the conviction that an injustice has been committed that must be corrected, by violence if necessary. It is too facile to argue in all or most of these cases that the people who resort to violence are not the genuine victims of outrageous injustice; often it seems they have no non-violent means to address the injustice.

St. Thomas Aquinas holds that justice is the highest of the moral virtues, and if he is right that justice is the most important temporal value, this might reveal precisely why the demand for justice can be so violent. As Christians we know, and the Catechism reminds us, that perfect justice is not attainable in this world before Christ's coming. If injustice is as inevitable an aspect of human life as human sin, and if injustice often leads to violence, and violence always leads to still more injustice, it is clear how easy it can be to get caught up in an unending spiral of injustice, anger, and violence.

Peace, both inner personal peace and world peace, demands that the desire for justice be tempered with love, mercy and forgiveness, even though it may sometimes seem "unjust" to forgive the oppressors. The hard truth of the cross is that at some point the cycle of violence and injustice has to stop, and it can only stop when someone freely chooses to take the pain and forgive. This is a miracle that is possible only through grace, and yet given the countless injustices and armaments of our world it is also strictly necessary if we are not to blow ourselves up.

Thus, ironically, although justice may be the highest human value of this world, if human beings cannot live and die for something that transcends the demands of justice, life in this world becomes impossible, and even more unjust. Justice connotes a certain impersonality, mutuality, and equality. Love, as revealed by Jesus, adds a crucial sacrificial and personal dimension, without which social life becomes unbearable and war inevitable.

Action on behalf of justice means demanding that human rights be respected. Love, and the desire for peace, mean that one may sometimes be called to give up one's rights. Finally, it is important to note that the decision to give up one's rights, if done well, may challenge the unjust status quo far more profoundly than a more conventional demand for justice.

Although the christological grounding of the moral life is evident in the Catechism, one wishes it had gone further, and called attention to the fact that Jesus inspired Gandhi, Martin Luther King Jr., and other great champions of human rights. They all made the personal, deliberate choice to place themselves in situations where they would be unjustly attacked and condemned by an oppressive power structure; through their voluntary acceptance of the unjust punishment by the system, they ultimately destroyed that very system. They have been given a life in eternity not granted to the principalities and powers who killed them. They showed that pacifism is not passive. This is active, creative, non-violence, which differs from nihilistic pacifism by affirming that while there is nothing worth killing for, there is something worth dying for. And it is here that the tension between justice and peace is ultimately healed through the power of love.

# THE HOMILY AND CATECHESIS: THE CATECHISM AND/OR THE LECTIONARY?

## Gerard S. Sloyan

First, a brief review of some recent history. The Second Council of the Vatican, in its Constitution on the Sacred Liturgy, *Sacrosanctum Concilium* (promulgated at the end of the second session on December 4, 1963), mandated among other things a new lectionary to replace the epistle and gospel readings of the *Missale Romanum* of 1570. These had been in use in the west since the early middle ages. The council fathers of Vatican II said: "The treasures of the Bible are to be opened up more lavishly, so that richer fare may be provided for the faithful at the table of God's word. In this way a more representative portion of the holy scriptures will be read to the people in the course of a prescribed number of years."

The only source I know of that describes the work of Study Group 11 of the post-conciliar Council [in Latin, *Consilium* with an "s"] for Following Up on the Constitution on the Sacred Liturgy is Chapter 26 of Archbishop Annibale Bugnini's *The Reform of the Liturgy, 1948–1975* (Collegeville, MN: Liturgical Press, 1983, pp. 406–25). Gaston Fontaine, a Canadian Canon Regular of the Immaculate Conception, had served the French-speaking bishops of his country as director of the liturgical movement there. As secretary of the post-conciliar Study Group in Rome throughout, he was one of the chief creators of the Lectionary for the Mass. He died in early 1992. Father Godfrey Diekmann of St. John's Abbey, Collegeville, who served as relator for the group in its first six months, knew him well. Entitled *The Revised Lectionary of the Roman Missal for Sundays and Solemnities,* the readings were introduced worldwide on the first Sunday of Advent, 1969, and made mandatory two years later. A two-year weekday lectionary accompanied it. The U.S. bishops introduced both on the earliest possible date.

The Sunday lectionary had been introduced upon its completion, "for experiment," in certain European churches but in no other regions of the world. The response that came back—I heard Father Fontaine say this at a gathering of Protestant liturgiologists in a Washington hotel a dozen years ago—was that the selections were too long. In effect: "You can never get Catholics to sit still for that much reading." As a result, the original selections from the Bible were much truncated by the time they reached the churches. This accounts for the shocking brevity of many pericopes, mainly the second readings from the epistolary literature (as an example, Romans 8:26–27 on Sunday 16, Year B). When the Bible is badly read, of course, congregations are grateful that the readings are short. On balance, however, the first two readings are an exercise in frustration.

I need not tell you that the three readings are keyed to each other thematically on Sundays, on the major feasts, and in Advent and Lent. On all Sundays and feasts the tone is set for the first reading by the readings from Matthew, Mark, and Luke, with readings from John interspersed. A selection is made from the First Testament in the measure that it foreshadows either the whole gospel reading or some phrase or phrases in it. This is the typological principle so beloved of the church fathers. A narrative or other genre of writing from the First Testament is declared a *typos* or *figura* of an event in Jesus' career, making him the "antitype." The technique is very ancient in Christian use, starting with the gospels themselves. The principle is easy to apply when a gospel passage echoes certain details in a story from the First Testament. Thus, for example, the feeding with loaves and fishes told twice in Mark at chapters 6 and 8 recalls the story of the manna in Exodus 16 and Numbers 11, but it especially echoes Elijah's feeding of one hundred people with twenty loaves of barley and fresh ears of grain in 2 Kings 4:42–44. The same is true of Jesus' three resuscitations of the dead and those told of Elijah and Elisha. But often the link between the first reading and the third will consist in no more than a word or a phrase. In those cases the typological element runs thin.

The second readings go their own way, except on major feasts and seasons as noted above. Paul's epistles and the others he did not write—Ephesians and the pastorals—while read semi-continuously, once begun are not read in the order of their occurrence in printed Bibles over the three-year period. Rather, some successive selections from Paul's longer and more substantive letters are read in each year (Romans, the Corinthian correspondence).

The interruption of the three synoptic gospels by Johannine pericopes in each year is a major problem, as all homilists and liturgy committees know. This and the recurrence of feasts and seasons with readings from gospels other than the one prescribed for the year make it hard to expound the Markan gospel or the Matthean or the Lukan, each with its special character and emphasis, until Pentecost is well over. The proposal for a four-year lectionary, which lost out in committee, is amply described in Archbishop Bugnini's chapter. I reckon the three-year lectionary rather than the four a major pastoral tragedy because of the violence it does to each of the gospels.

In 1981 the list of readings was revised but not very much. The revision has not been promulgated in this country and this is not a matter of loss. Extensive revision is being called for from every side after twenty-five years. No Roman response has been forthcoming.

## TOWARD A COMMON LECTIONARY?

Some American Protestants began to use the Catholic lectionary as early as 1970. In 1977 the Episcopal Church in this country produced a revision of *The Book of Common Prayer* for use beginning in 1978. It has a three-year lectionary patterned on the Roman, but retaining some Anglican calendar features from the days of Cranmer and Laud, and some special U.S. features. That committee began and ended certain Roman readings at different verses. At times they chose different First Testament readings as better upholding the typological principle. There was no direct consultation with Catholic lectionary experts, not out of ill will but because the benefits to our larger communion and their smaller one probably did not occur to them. The liturgiologists and the Bible experts in most churches are usually not the ecumenists. Besides, as the U.S. Episcopal Church well knew, with the Catholics going lockstep as we do worldwide, we had no freedom to negotiate.

In 1980 five Lutheran synods in this country and Canada, including the Missouri but not the Wisconsin, produced jointly a *Book of Worship*. It contains a three-year lectionary. That committee consulted neither Episcopal nor Catholic *periti*, while taking guidance from the lectionaries of both. Again, understandably, certain Lutheran calendar traditions were adhered to, which resulted in the readings frequently being "off" from the Roman by one week or two. Some theological convictions from the reformation also had a part in the inclusion or exclusion of certain pericopes.

In 1983 a Protestant group that had Catholic consultors, the Consultation on Common Texts, produced a *Common Lectionary*. It, too, derived from the Roman but was distinguished by its copious use of First Testament readings that did *not* go on the typological principle. The reasons were two. The framers wished to avoid portraying Israel as a religion of the past supplanted by Christianity, as an exclusively typological reading of its scriptures tends to suggest. Further, they were convinced that worshipers in the lectionary churches were being deprived of many rich narratives and writings of the prophets by the determining force the gospels have on First Testament selections. Incidentally, the *Common Lectionary* follows the Episcopal Lectionary in providing for alternate readings from the deuterocanonical books on the days the Roman Lectionary proposes them as the only reading.

At the appearance of the *Common Lectionary* in 1983, the Presbyterians, United Church of Christ, and Disciples of Christ abandoned the lectionaries each had developed on the pattern of the Roman in favor of the Common. The United Methodists, three African-American Methodist churches, and the Community Churches did the same. Those last eight plus the Episcopal Church all belong to the Consultation on Church Union (renamed the Church of Christ Uniting). At that point the committee of U.S. bishops on the liturgy asked the Roman See if selected churches in this country could use the *Common Lectionary ad experimentum*. I saw the letter of refusal from a curial cardinal. The practice would be disruptive of western Catholic unity worldwide, they were told. Besides, the *Common Lectionary* did not admit the disputed books of the longer canon—which was not true.

The *Common Lectionary* came out in a much revised form in 1992 and would be a splendid candidate for all the churches in the U.S. and Canada, including our own. Consider the sign of unity twelve or fifteen North American communions would constitute, praying and preaching the same Bible readings every Sunday. I predict it will come about once our bishops begin to take ecumenism seriously. Shrinking numbers at Sunday worship in all but the evangelical churches will force them into an ecumenical posture they have, until now, had the luxury to abstain from.

## THE LECTIONARY IN WORSHIP

There is no need for me to review here the aspects of lectionary use that clergy and people complain about. A sample will do: "Who knows why these (or those) readings were chosen?"; "No one can preach on three readings that go in three directions or even two"; "The people are simply mystified by the history and place names of the Old Testament"; "Congregation members need to hear more of the basic truths of faith and less of Jeremiah's woes or Paul's travels." You have heard it all. Another set of complaints needs to be taken seriously, for that first list does little more than testify to clergy unwillingness to do hard Bible study and reflection. I reckon as legitimate complaints the following: between the mumblers of both sexes, the soft feminine voices, the droners, the sing-songers, and those who do not project their voices, you cannot *hear* them (number one by all odds); the priests and deacons do not preach on the Bible readings, or if they do they repeat what the gospel just said and far less elegantly; the most interesting homilists give you something to think about but it bears little relation to the "richer fare at the table of God's word" promised by the Constitution on the Sacred Liturgy.

In spite of this chorus of woes, the fact is that Catholic public reading and preaching is far better today than it was in 1963. There are more people in the pews who know what to listen for in the Bible than there were then. There are more homilists working at their preaching, which means chiefly probing the Bible readings before they presume to speak about them. Fewer people are coming to the Sunday eucharist, it is true, but the ones who come are those who by and large wish to be there.

The purpose of liturgy, of which Bible reading and commentary upon it are an integral part, is prayer. It is the church's public prayer. The sacraments are not a system, not an "economy." They are the variety of ways in which the church prays publicly. The liturgy of the hours is one of those ways. It is in the setting of the daily eucharist that only a few have the opportunity to pray. But the parishes that provide it for ten or fifteen regulars say they will never be the same. Any private prayer Christians may engage in is a boon, a grace to them. It is especially a good of the church because it helps them, and all who benefit from their prayer participate more fully in the rest of the church's prayer.

When the church prays publicly, instruction is certainly admissible as part of that prayer. The whole rite, any rite, instructs. It cannot not do so. The Bible reading and the homily are not alone in this formative function but are joined by the whole text of the rite; the bodily movements of people and ministers; the music of song and its lyrics, provided they are good religious poetry and not banal; the vesture; the appointments of the worship space; yes and even the smoke of burning incense that rises to the Lord. Liturgy is simply formative of Christian life as the east has known for centuries and the west is slowly coming to learn. Liturgy is chiefly worship, the prayer of the community. While it instructs it does so only incidentally. It is intended to worship, to give thanks, to ask, to plead, to importune. The lectionary readings and the homily are not an instructive interlude in worship. They *are* worship, worshipful words. They are a treasure of Christian life if, in the homily, used sparingly.

Catechesis is chiefly instruction. It should always be engaged in prayerfully. Only privileged populations are catechized: the young, whether by the adults in their household or by others like you in formal classes; new candidates for Christian life. The latter are the lucky ones, since the period of their gestation in Christ is often superior to life outside the baptismal womb. Some adults too, never in large numbers, receive the catechesis that their zeal and their years deserve: in Bible study groups; in lecture series; in academic courses in the parishes that sponsor them.

## CATECHISTS AND THE LECTIONARY

There is a movement abroad of which some of you have heard, called lectionary catechesis. I do not favor it. I think it confuses two different types of Christian formation. At its best it ties formal instruction to the biblical texts of public prayer. At its worst it is an attempt to salvage hopelessly bad Sunday liturgies, which are the bane of a catechist's life. Mind you, I am not speaking against lectionary study by RCIA candidates. I am opposed to doing in one medium what should be happening in another. Exhorting, inviting, preparing for better preaching and celebrating is only to be praised, provided that catechists stay faithful to their didactic task.

Catechizing and lectionary proclamation in tandem make eminent sense. The catechism *or* the lectionary is a false dichotomy and makes little sense. The best catechesis I know is formal Bible study—of both Testaments and for all ages. It is the optimum preparation for partaking in public worship. But it is no substitute for it. Catechists can serve a particular worshiping community by helping its readers read well and its ministers minister well and its ushers usher well. "Oh, but the liturgy committee does that!" it may be objected. Or, "The director of song would not be pleased by an analysis of the soupy, sappy lyrics proposed to a victim congregation." Or, "The clergy have us boxed in at every turn." Catechists are educators, religious educators. Among other tasks, they do all in their power to get people ready for public prayer. They do not describe to people, young or old, what happens in the church's prayer. If the liturgy itself does not do that, no words can achieve it.

Catechists are formal teachers by calling who seize every opportunity. Seizing a sizable portion of the church bulletin is an excellent idea. As with all journalism its white space needs filling regularly, intelligent filling—teaching, in other words. Short quotations from books and articles, fully acknowledged, are a place to start. The use of excerpts from the catechism under consideration qualifies only rarely. What can be done in print is expounding the Sunday readings exegetically in a way that has no place in the pulpit. The monthly feature "Studying the Lectionary" in the Liturgical Conference's *Homily Service* is the best resource I know, and permission to reprint is freely given.

## WHAT CAN THE CATECHISM DO FOR LITURGY?

I must turn briefly to what this catechism can do for liturgy— not just for biblical proclamation and preaching but for liturgy in its totality. The answer is not very much unless one laboriously mines its treatment of the sacraments, which of course are liturgy. Part Four on prayer, for all its virtues, is mostly about the prayer of individuals. All very important. Only individuals pray in concert. But the focus is on single ones more than on any concerted action in prayer, which is what the liturgy is. In the midst of the discussion (§§ 2653–60), a heading "On the Sources of Prayer" proposes the Holy Spirit as the living water that leaps up to everlasting life in the praying heart (Jn 4:14). Fair enough. Who else could be considered the author of our prayer? Then there come in order paragraphs on the word of God, meaning a frequent and prayerful reading of the Bible (§ 2653), the church's liturgy—a paragraph of six lines (§ 2655) that speaks of the human heart as an altar. "Prayer interiorizes and assimilates the liturgy during and after its celebration"—one suspects, in the context, more after than during. Christians enter into prayer as they enter into liturgy (I paraphrase) in a spirit of faith, hope, and love. We seek, we desire the face of the Lord, we wish to hear and treasure his word through the signs of his presence (§ 2656).

In the earlier treatment of the sacrament of the eucharist, which consumes ninety-eight numbered paragraphs spread over thirty pages, the "liturgy of the word" is described as following the assembly of the faithful. It is followed in turn by the presentation of the gifts (still called "the offertory" in parentheses), the *collecta*, the anaphora with its constituent parts, and the communion. The liturgy of the word is described as readings from both Testaments followed by a homily that exhorts hearers to receive this word for what it truly is, the word of God (1 Thessalonians 2:13 is here appositely cited), and to put it into practice. That certainly is the function of the service of the word: not a dull didacticism but a renewed invitation to life.

Having pointed this out, can I direct readers to any other place in *Catéchisme* where lectionary speaks to catechesis or catechesis to lectionary? There is one other and it is spread throughout the book. Public readers, homilists, and liturgy planners might all do well to mark up their copies or even make extracts of some extraordinarily beautiful quotations. These come from the fathers, from saints of both sexes, and from eastern liturgies (not "Orthodox" because they all pre-date the division). Some of the better prayers of the western liturgy are a puzzling absentee. The fathers are quoted as saying some prosaic things as well, scarcely worth repeating in a solemn tone. But quite a good anthology can be culled from the Catechism for use in the proclamation of the word.

I do not propose that homilists use *Catéchisme* otherwise as a source for public reflection on the scriptures. The revelation of the apostolic age as subsequently developed can be found much better expressed in other sources that have a sense of history. A good theological education should have told people where to go if they wish to elaborate on a particular mystery of faith. A good theological dictionary should be at hand, likewise the *Oxford Dictionary of the Christian Church,* and any and all publications of Liturgy Training Publications of Chicago and the Liturgical Conference of Silver Spring, MD.

Preaching on the lectionary has as its chief purpose exhortation, as the catechism says. Paradoxically, the best exhorters in the pulpit are those who teach. The direct exhorters are masters of the MEGO: "My eyes glaze over." Occasionally, from a liturgical text like a lectionary phrase a demand for catechesis will flow. Homilists should stand ready to provide it in brief and succinct fashion. But the two ways of carrying on formation in Christ should not be confused. Catechesis should not preempt the lectionary's function. The lectionary and homilies upon it may be informal but never formal occasions for catechesis.

Any proposal to divide up the Catechism as the subject of pulpit instruction during the eucharistic celebration is to be deplored utterly. Such a program understands neither liturgy nor catechesis. It would be to rob Catholics of their biblical heritage yet again and only doubtfully instruct them.

# CULTURAL PLURALISM AND THE CATECHISM

## Virgil Elizondo

I begin with a personal note. I come to you first of all as a fellow catechist who has taught every level of catechesis from pre-school to university. I have been professionally involved in catechetics since 1967 when I participated in the International Study Week of Catechetics in the East Asian Pastoral Institute and Medellín Catechetical Study Week of 1968 and have continued to be involved in catechetics since then in various ways.

I also come to you as a pastor of a very active parish who is learning that the more local we are, the more universal we become. We televise a Sunday liturgy to the entire nation. It is a very Mexican celebration. Yet the appeal of this mass is far beyond the Hispanics of the United States. Our growing audience (millions each week) includes peoples of all ethnic backgrounds and even of other denominations. We are also discovering that the more traditional we are, the more contemporary we become. This is the very paradox of church: local yet universal, traditional yet contemporary. The church is not an either/or, but the mystery of the unity of the past with the present, the particular with the absolute, and the finite with the infinite.

Finally, I come to you with the experience of the last twenty years of pioneering inter-cultural ministry through the work of the Mexican American Cultural Center in San Antonio. We are discovering more and more that ethnic, cultural, and racial diversity is not a curse to be avoided or a problem to be solved, but a challenge for the rehabilitation of God's broken and wounded humanity. It is in fact the great challenge and opportunity for the build-up of a radically new human community such as the world has never known. Either we work toward this new community, or we all face the danger of ethnic annihilation together. I look to the *Catechism of the Catholic Church* as potentially a great tool to help us in the build-up of this new inter-cultural and pluri-cultural community.

Those who were expecting a world catechism that would be the same for everyone everywhere in the globe, one that simply needs to be translated into the local languages, simplified and illustrated, will find the new Catechism a terrific disappointment. Whereas everyone is invited to read it, the *Catechism of the Catholic Church* (*CCC*) is primarily a guide book for bishops and catechetical leaders to serve them as a reference point in their ministry of expounding and clarifying the Christian mysteries. It is like the grammar book—not the grammar that will create an artificial and unnatural language, but one that has been carefully discerned and systematized out of the people's living language of faith. One might also say that the *CCC* is like the dictionary—nobody goes to the dictionary to study literature, but it helps to clarify and bring out the exact meaning of the stories and adventures of literature. Native speakers can be quite fluent in their language before studying the grammar but the grammar nonetheless enriches and guides their use of the language. The message is not in the dictionary or the grammar but in the literature. So, the Catechism might well be described as the grammar and dictionary of the living faith language and culture of the Catholic faithful in their living tradition of nearly two thousand years. The great challenge for local catechetical teams will be to produce catechisms that will be both grammatically correct and as substantially exciting as a good novel—in message, stories, illustrations, style, ordering. The more that this is so, the more that each catechism will be at one and the same time very particular and very universal, faithful to the local people for whom it is composed and faithful to what the Catholic Church teaches for all.

John Paul II states in the apostolic constitution *Fidei depositum* that this *Catechism of the Catholic Church* is the product of the various consultations throughout the entire church over a period of several years. It represents and pulls together the collective wisdom of the past and the present. The process, though not perfect and to everyone's satisfaction, made it possible for a good sample of the *sensus fidelium* to emerge. The *CCC* collates and presents what has become most basic across the centuries and yet it itself does not tire in pointing to the one indispensable and unchanging basis of faith and unity: the Lordship of the crucified Jesus of Nazareth.

My assignment is to look at the *CCC* from the perspective of cultural pluralism. After a preliminary sketch of the notion of diversity, I shall proceed in two sections: (1) textual highlights of the Catechism that explicitly bring out the necessity of diversity in various areas of the church's life, and (2) our challenge for the future, or "where do we go from here?" It is a challenging and exciting task. The innermost questions of culture and religion are among the deepest, most devastating, and most ancient questions plaguing today's world. They appear as the greatest obstacles to peace and unity among peoples. Yet these very same questions and historical tensions equally present the greatest potential for a new world vision and structure wherein diversity will not be seen as a curse to be eliminated, but a blessing to be assumed and appreciated. Because the church is in the world, the world's questions and its struggles are the questions and struggles of the church. To balance diverse religious expression and unity of faith is one of the most intriguing and fascinating challenges for today's global and local church.

## PRELIMINARY OBSERVATIONS ON CULTURAL PLURALISM

Cultural pluralism is not several cultures simply living next to each other tolerating one another (at best). It is not one dominant and normative culture that allows the folkloric and subalternate presence of others—especially those that it cannot avoid or keep out. It is not every group simply doing its own thing.

Cultural pluralism is the modern day phenomenon of several cultures/races co-existing together in the same geographical space and participating actively in the same political/economic state and even in the same religious assemblies. This is the reality of countries like the United States, France, England, Australia, and a few others. Various peoples are becoming part of the whole without giving up the essential elements of their ancestral cultural/religious identity. For this to take place without introducing new divisions, it is necessary to relativize certain elements of each culture while sharpening the innermost spirit that can mobilize the various peoples/cultures/races into "one people"—one people of God. Given the multi-cultural reality of the United States, this will be a very special and unique challenge to the church of our country.

Today, the right to be oneself, that is, "to be other," is being recognized as a fundamental human right. Culturally speaking, there is no human group—ethnic, civic, or religious—that can hold claim to being the absolute and normative model for all others. Everyone is being called to a new humility and to a new awareness of how much we can learn from one another. Today we are seeking to build paradigms on the "and/and" model, which seeks to harmonize differences for the betterment of everyone. Differences can be seen more in terms of complementarity than by way of opposition. This makes of every other and their otherness a potential friend, collaborator, and source of enrichment.

## PURPOSE AND INTENT OF THE *CCC*

The *Catechism of the Catholic Church* is definitely not intended to be a universal catechism in the sense that one catechetical text will serve the needs of every place in the world for all time. In *Depositum fidei,* Pope John Paul II emphasizes twice that the Catechism is intended as a *reference text* for the *catechisms and compendia* that are *to be composed* (not translated!) in the *diverse countries.* He goes on to state that it is not intended to replace local catechisms but rather to encourage and help redaction of local catechisms, which are aware of diverse situations and cultures while guarding unity of faith and fidelity to Catholic doctrine. (The emphases are my own.)

In its very opening statements the *CCC* itself states clearly that it is "destined to serve as a point of reference for the elaboration of catechisms or compendia in diverse countries" (§ 11). It does not say that it is simply to be translated and used with all peoples everywhere. It invites anyone who is interested to read it, but the document is primarily intended for bishops and those responsible for catechetics:

> Let no one imagine that only one kind of souls are confined to
> their care and hence are to teach all the faithful in the same

way. . . . The words should be carefully chosen according to the
spirit and intelligence of the audience (§ 24).

We might say that the *Catechism of the Catholic Church* is to be
like the skeleton that is to be thoroughly enfleshed in each local
church.[1] Since it refers to itself as a reference point, we might well
liken it to the architectural principles elaborated by the magisterium
after having listened carefully to the people of God. These principles are needed for the creative architect to produce the blueprint—
considering the local terrain, climate, history, and present reality.
This will be the task of the catechetical team of the local (regional)
church. The publishers will be the builders, while the local pastors
and catechists will be the construction workers that will build up
the local edifice of God's kingdom in this specific locality and in
this precise moment of time (the challenge of the local pastors
and catechists). The diversity of the local churches, with their traditions, liturgies, catechisms, spiritualities, and theologies, is an earthly image of the Father's house in which there are many mansions
(not utility apartments, that look all the same and boring), but no
division whatsoever.

## DIVERSITY: GIFT OR CURSE

*Diversity of Peoples as a Fact of Life.* Diversity and similarity of
individuals, of families, of groups, of nations, and of races is the
obvious fact of human existence. All humanity is one, but there
are no two individuals—even identical twins—who are exactly the
same in everything. Because we are human and in order to be human, we seek to socialize. From our earliest beginnings, we seek the
company of those we recognize as our own and are afraid of the
unknown other—a baby cries spontaneously when an unknown
person approaches and presents a potential danger. We are comfortable with our own, but threatened by the other to the degree
that our defense mechanisms are alerted as the other approaches.
Even if the stranger is appealing to us, we are still uncomfortable
and defensive because of his/her otherness. In ordinary life, the
other is first perceived as danger rather than as friend. This is true
whether at the level of individuals, families, classes, nations, or races.
This deep human instinct is reinforced by the religious beliefs

that inform the deepest levels of the human psyche—both personal and collective.

Even though migrations and the mixing of peoples (*mestizaje*) have taken place since time immemorial, cultural identity has frequently been intimately associated with the race, geographical place, and historical pilgrimage of a people. In many ways, the "nation" was "the people," that is, the cultural synthesis of the various forces that had led the people to be who they are here and now in this time and space. The collective soul of the people has been gradually formulated and expressed through the customs, foods, language, values, artistic forms, and religious expression of the people. Others who today come into this space and time are foreigners and immigrants.

Today, the world of nations is changing very rapidly. Twenty-six nationalities make up one small village in northern France, and their children are all growing up "French" and "other" at the same time. The children of the Spanish migrant workers in France and in England are growing up "French-Spanish" or "English-Spanish," the children of the Ethiopians in Italy are growing up "Italian-Ethiopian," the children of the Japanese in Brazil are truly Brazilian-Japanese, and we could go on *ad infinitum*. Migrations and the mixture of peoples are taking place throughout the globe, and even though they might live in ethnic ghettos for a while, a newness begins to emerge in the children. Nowhere is this taking place more rapidly than in the United States. We are truly a multi-ethnic and multi-racial nation. We are a people of many peoples. We struggle with many unresolved problems of linguistics, racism, and ethnicity, yet our ongoing challenge is to grow even stronger as a united people. The future of the United States is in the diversity of its peoples; its curse is special interest groups that subvert the common good for the sake of their own profit and gain.

An even more astounding development is the growing awareness within the church of the positive values of all religions. We are becoming more aware of the great variety of religions in the world and of the great variety of religious expressions and teachings within each religious group. Religions should not be out to eliminate one another but to enrich one another. This has certainly been my personal experience—the more I learn about other religions, the more I deepen and expand the appreciation of my own

Christian Catholic tradition. And even our own Latin (Roman) Catholicism is certainly not monolithic. There is great variety and diversity even within a given diocese, parish, or religious community.

## HIGHLIGHTS OF THE *CCC*

The *Catechism of the Catholic Church* is to be implemented within the context of the living faith, that is, within the historical and cultural reality of the people. The church in its great tradition has fostered diversity much more than conformity and in so doing has brought about the great unity of the Spirit that started at Pentecost. Historically, to the degree that the church becomes defensive and tries to impose uniformity from on high, it ends up bringing about the very opposite of what it intends: division.[2] The gospels themselves are a good example of a pluriform catechetical text: we have only one Jesus of Nazareth, but there are four diverse accounts of his life and ministry. The entire *CCC* emphasizes the enriching role of diversity and insists on the elaboration of texts for diverse countries. We could add that, given the actual situation of most of the Catholic countries of the west, and especially the United States, not only will there be different catechisms for different countries, but quite diverse catechisms within a given country, and even more so, a genuine pluriformity within each of the diverse catechisms. This is the social reality of these countries, and this is the reality out of which the church must reach out in its catechesis. Here are some especially important texts in the *CCC*.

## FOUNDATIONAL IMAGE OF GOD'S INTENT AND HUMANITY'S EVIL (§§ 56–58)

The great diversity of the peoples as created by God (Gen 10) stands in complete contrast to sinful humanity's empires of uniformity (Gen 11). In the second creation (after the deluge), God blessed Noah and told him to multiply and fill the earth (Gen 9). God made a covenant with Noah. The sign of that covenant was the rainbow—the beauty of unity in diversity from beginning to end. The result of that blessing (Gen 10) was the great diversity of families, peoples, languages, and nations that filled the earth. Each one in its uniqueness radiated a portion of God's glory, but no one nation alone revealed the fullness of God's glory. God did this, according to the *CCC,* to keep any one nation from becoming too proud, thus thinking that it was self-sufficient and without need of God or of others. Diversity of peoples is the creator's great gift, and their harmonious unity is the creator's great glory. Paragraphs 337, 341, and 361 elaborate on the positive value and beauty of diversity as created and intended by God.

Paragraph 57 brings out that sinful human beings will choose a totally different type of unity than the one intended by God. As in the beginning, humanity constantly prefers its own way to God's. In Genesis 11, humanity wants to make its way to God in its own way by building a city with a tower: an image of one uniform and totalitarian way of life for everyone. Thus one people's way of life will appear as God's own way, and this people will set themselves up against all others. They will not just be different, but superior. Once people set themselves up as the exclusive image of the values, the beauty, and the greatness of God, they make of themselves an idol! Sinful humanity now becomes united "only in its perverse ambition to forge its own unity as in the tower of Babel" (§ 57)— a forced and idolatrous uniformity for everyone. This is the great evil of the world—to set ourselves up as the measure of good and evil of all others! We become normative and judgmental. In this sinful condition, even in trying to do good for others, we often end up destroying their inner soul. As any nation can easily become an idol, so can any local church when it sets itself up as the norm for all others.

Unconsciously and certainly not maliciously, the Euro-North American church has functioned in this way in relation to the local churches of the rest of the world. Since Vatican II, things have started to change, but it is not easy to change an unquestioned practice of centuries. A rediscovery of the tradition of the church is helping to bring this about. However, the temptation will always be there to make of our own cultural, national, or ecclesial expression the idol that will become the norm for all others.

"There is no single aspect of the Christian message that is not in part an answer to the question of evil" (§ 309). We have to unveil the specific manifestations of evil in our society. The false sense of superiority and righteousness of some cultures and some churches that justifies multi-faceted racism, sexism, classism, ethno-centrism, ecclesio-centrism, religio-centrism, and other forms of human degradation and marginalization is the great evil of today's world. It is this righteous sense of superiority that has enabled so-called Christians and a civilization that called itself Christian[3] to conquer entire peoples, steal their lands, enslave their people, exploit their natural resources, underpay their workers, and destroy entire ways of life that were sacred to the peoples of the land. Those defined as "unwanted/untouchable" by the dominant groups are still kept out of the structures of responsibility and opportunity on a wholesale basis—even out of the priesthood and religious life. This great evil still persists and often goes unquestioned and unchallenged by the catechists and theologians of the more powerful Christian churches. The entire Christian message must be understood and proclaimed as radically opposing this evil, which continues to cause so much pain and misery to the masses of the world. This evil denies the fundamental dignity of the human person in his/her historical and cultural reality.

## BEGINNING OF NEW CREATION:
## SON OF GOD BECOMES HUMAN FLESH

The very particular and historically and culturally conditioned Jesus of Nazareth becomes the universal savior of humanity. The section on the Son of God (§§ 426ff) brings out clearly what is repeated in various ways throughout the document, that Jesus of Nazareth is the heart of all catechesis. Without question, this entire section places Jesus among the poor, the lowly, the marginalized and the ridiculed of society—"the king of glory rides on a donkey" (§ 559). The glory of God's own Son "is hidden in the weakness of the new-born baby" (§ 563). When he was born, people had no room for him or his parents. Throughout his life he associated with the public sinners (social outcasts) and untouchables of his own people. In the end, his sufferings "took their historical and concrete form in the fact that he was rejected and handed over" (§ 572). From his conception to his death on the cross, Jesus is without doubt "the stone rejected by the builders of this world" (Acts 4:11).

Yet, precisely out of the evil of marginalization and rejection, the marginal Jesus of Nazareth dares to live and proclaim a new human alternative: the reign of God who is love unlimited and who invites us to a life of love, forgiveness, fellowship, and self-sacrifice for the sake of others. This love will destroy all barriers that keep people apart, whether they are racial, sexual, ethnic, religious, or moral, and will heal the wounds of those whom society has humiliated, disregarded, ignored, judged as "public sinners," and unwanted except when they need to be enslaved and exploited (§ 544).

The table fellowship of Jesus to which all are welcomed is the very particular, real, and concrete beginning of the new divine alternative to humanity's multiple divisions. The holiness of Jesus comes through in the fact that, like his Father, he welcomes everyone without exception—especially the most disliked and unwanted of society and religion. Everyone is invited not just to follow him, but to become a body and blood member of his family! For this, he will give his own body and blood so that the cosmic body will no longer be ripped apart by our human arrogance and the divisions caused by it.

It is important to note the privileged role of the poor and the outcasts of Jesus' own culture and religion. These people continue to have a privileged role in every culture that receives Christianity. The dominant culture must be questioned and challenged from their perspective (§ 1676). The marginal of the dominant culture are the first ones to hear and receive the word and through their popular piety and rites truly make it their own. It is among them that God's new alternative for society begins.

## THE HOLY SPIRIT: THE CHURCH

*Disciples.* The people of God assembling together throughout the world (§ 752) is the fruit of the Spirit. The church is sent to make disciples within all nations (§ 767), that is, to enable persons to see themselves and others in a radically new way: as accepted, respected, and loved by God. God's accepting love heals the deep wounds of segregation and rejection. The disciple is one who breaks through the dehumanizing prejudices and sees the beauty, dignity, and truth of oneself and the others as God sees us: all children of the same God, all equal members of the same family. The disciple does not abandon the heritage or religious expression of his/her ancestors, but begins to live it in a new way.

Discipleship affirms the local culture while destroying its prejudices and fears of others. That is precisely why the church is such a complex reality (§ 771): it is the mystery of the intimate unity with God of all peoples and therefore the intimate unity of the human race, of all the peoples of all nations, races, and languages. Thus the church is both the instrumental beginning of that unity and the great sign of the ultimate unity that is yet to be accomplished (§ 775). The original covenant with Noah is brought to perfection: not just coexistence of nations, but a new loving fellowship.

While all nations/cultures are invited to become disciples, "God does not belong to any one nation or people" (§ 782). By consequence, we can say that God does not belong to any one local church of a given country. No one local church exhausts the mystery of God, and no local church is superior to or better than the others. Each one has a legitimate and beautiful uniqueness while being united with all the others in the one spirit that allows us all to confess that the crucified Jesus of Nazareth is the Lord. The Holy Father "presides over the whole assembly of charity and protects legitimate differences, while at the same time such differences do not hinder unity but rather contribute to it" (*Lumen Gentium* 13).

*The Universality of the Church.* In view of the evil of the world, what makes us "a holy nation" (§ 803; 1 Pet 2:9) is precisely our refusal to reject anyone and our openness to the otherness of the other. The reason for this is the very foundation of the church: the Holy Trinity, which is the ultimate source of God's life—unity in diversity (§ 814). Because of this, the very catholicity of the church, its innermost universality, which exists at the core of every local church, is precisely its ability to take root in any of the cultures of the world (§ 835). This inner attitude of being big enough to be able to take in anyone and everyone is the universal life and spirit of the church.

This is precisely why any effort to impose a superficial or even intellectual uniformity is such an incredible assault on the most beautiful aspect of the church: its innermost catholicity. It is this spirit of a positive prejudice in favor of the otherness of the others that distinguishes the church universally. Its desire to discover and appreciate the positive elements of other peoples and other religions is a result of its universal love of God's very diverse creation. The universality of the church does not erase differences nor bring about a uniform humanity. In the power of the one Spirit of unlimited love, the particular (without ceasing to be particular) now has universal implications in that it welcomes others universally. This is the one universal and universalizing element of the church—not that it is the same everywhere and at all times, but that it now has a big enough heart and mind to love everyone as they are!

*The Particularity of the Universal.*[4] In Christian language, the word "church" is used for the liturgical assembly, the local community, and the universal community of believers. These three meanings are inseparable. The church is the people of God assembled and realized throughout the world. It exists in the local communities and is realized as a liturgical community, especially in the eucharist (§ 752). The *CCC* goes on to state: "The great richness of their diversity is not opposed to the unity of the church" (§ 814). The healthy tension between the particular historical-cultural ecclesial expression and the universal tradition of the church will enhance the unity of the Spirit, which is so totally different and opposed to the idolatrous uniformity of the dominant of this world.

The church is the sacrament of Christ, and sacraments are "signs perceptible by the senses" (§ 1070). We know that the signs are perceived quite differently by different cultures. That is why in the celebration (liturgy) and explanation (catechesis) of the Christian mystery, so much careful attention has to be placed on the local history and culture. The creative composition of local catechisms that utilize the language, wisdom, and iconography of the people and that is attentive to the particular needs and problematic of the area is a fundamental task of the local church (§ 1075). This implies much more creative elaboration than a mere translation of the Catechism. As the Synod on Catechesis of 1977 points out:

> The real incarnation of the faith through catechesis involves not just the process of giving but also that of receiving. This means that not only must there be a process by which the faith

transforms and purifies culture, but there also has to be a process
by which the very faith itself has to be rethought and reinter-
preted.... In this sense, cultures themselves must discharge the
function of hermeneutic criterion in regard to the faith.[5]

The local catechism is to become one of the chief tools of the
ongoing inculturation of the church, thus allowing the life and
tradition of the church to become incarnate in this particular
people. Catechesis and culture are intimately and mutually inter-
dependent within the process of the growth and maturation of the
local church.

> Good theology is culturally and historically transcending only
> by its fidelity to its own particularity. Good catechisms are good
> by their fidelity to the same paradox of transcendence through
> the common confession rendered in distinct ways for distinct
> cultures. No one needs to become European to join "the world."
> No one should be expected to become European to join their
> narrative, their culture, their particularity to Jesus Christ and
> his culture-transcending (but not ignoring) church.[6]

The liturgy cannot just be taken from one place to the other.
It has to be enhanced by "the cultural richness belonging to God's
people who are celebrating." There has to be a "harmony of signs"
(§ 1158). Hence the music, the words, the artistic decorations, the
bodily motions and postures must be congruent with local variations. Without becoming just another festival of the people, the
liturgy must be in tune with a people's natural way of celebrating
and their style must be incorporated creatively into the liturgy so
that it is truly a liturgy of the people. Different moments of the liturgy will have different emphasis for different peoples. For example, in the eastern churches the entire holy week is celebrated as
"the great week" (§ 1169). This is similar to our Latin American
tradition of celebrating in a very special way the *la semana mayor.*
The celebration of Easter (§ 1169) on different dates by the great
traditions of the church is not just a mistake of the calendar, but
has diverse historical/theological reasons behind it.[7] Liturgists have
heart attacks with the Mexican Catholics, for whom the Feast of
Our Lady of Guadalupe is of far greater historical/liturgical importance than a Sunday of Advent, but the people consider the

liturgists to be totally irreverent and ignorant of the salvation history of the Mexican people when they cannot recognize this fact.

The authentic inculturation of liturgical celebration is much deeper and implies much more than just singing in the local language and using local material for the vestments. It implies a deep respect and willingness to walk with the people's faith pilgrimage with the full liturgical celebration of the special events that have marked their life and that form part of their collective memory. Catechetics needs to help in the creation of the local tradition of living faith. These local and particular liturgical customs develop as the faith tradition of the church gradually dialogues with the local culture and traditions of the people. In this process, there will be a mutual interpretation and enrichment of both the tradition and the new and developing local tradition. The cultural diversity of liturgical celebration that will emerge is a great source of enrichment that will continue to deepen, enlarge, and expand the innermost catholicity of the church (§§ 1203–1206).

Book II, Section 2.4 of the Catechism is entitled "Other Liturgical Celebrations." The title itself is quite fascinating because it places sacramentals and the popular faith among the liturgical celebrations of the church. The very title gives a new understanding of the relationship between sacraments, sacramentals, and popular expressions of faith. We have been accustomed to thinking of the sacraments as "the real thing" and the rest as something we could just as easily do without. But the Catechism appears to reject this notion in favor of greater complementarity.

The sections on sacramentals and popular piety are most important. This is probably the area through which inculturation takes place in the most natural and effective way. The reason for this is that "sacramentals respond to the needs of the culture and history of the particular regions and time" (§ 1668) and they arise from the priesthood of the baptized (§ 1669). This means that they arise out of the genius and needs of the people of faith, who are impelled by the Spirit to express and celebrate their Christian faith in ways that are totally natural to them. Since the people are not encumbered with the many studies that unfortunately remove the professional minister from the ordinary faithful, their expressions of faith can more easily come from the collective heart and mind of the people of God in this particular region. From the perspective of authentic inculturation, I would dare to say that these are the purest expressions of the faith in the local church. I am not saying that they are perfect, but definitely that they are neither false nor inferior to the liturgical forms that are all too often still imposed by outsiders of the particular local church. In these celebrations, everyone participates equally—laity and clergy, men and women, theologians and the simple faithful.

The Catechism makes its own the richest section of the Puebla Document of 1979 in the area of popular piety (§ 1674) designating the popular piety of the people as the chief criterion for discerning whether the gospel is being served or not:

> For the common people this wisdom (of popular religiosity) is also a principle of discernment and an evangelical instinct through which they spontaneously sense when the gospel is served in the church and when it is emptied of its content and stifled by other interests.[8]

The section on "Life in the Spirit" (beginning in § 1699) brings up more questions that can only be answered adequately in the local cultural setting. The notions of good/evil, right conscience, truth, obligation, law, etc. all have very different connotations in different cultures and historical situations. This is also true of the entire section on the ten commandments. Which interpretations are cultural, having to do with the western assumptions of the individual right to private property versus the collective ownership of this portion of the earth by a particular tribe or nation? Many such questions will come up and can only be answered by the moralists of the local church. Other aspects of morality, because of particular circumstances, will have more urgency and importance in some regions than in others. This is an excellent place for each group to develop a listing of the particular "cultural sins" that are destructive of this local people. For example, in the United States, I would consider upward mobility without limits one of the deepest idols and cultural sins, often accompanied by an extreme individualism that is not concerned with the common good, the poor, and the foreigner. Each human group has its own cultural sins that are destructive of life and of human dignity. These must be faced honestly by local catechisms.

The final section of the *CCC* (§§ 2587ff) deals with prayer. Prayer forms vary with local history and culture—an example of this is the Psalms themselves. Inspired songs and dances come out of the deepest spiritual recesses of a people. The native and African Americans have marvelous forms of prayer that can certainly enrich all of us. One form of prayer should not be imposed on the others, but a variety of forms can enrich everyone. For many of my people at San Fernando Cathedral, the lighting of a simple vigil light comes through as a truly mystical experience. Many of our old *viejitas* are masters of contemplation and mysticism. We have so much to learn from them. For a very good example of this, I suggest a careful reading of Victor Villaseñor's classic book, *Rain of Gold.*[9] The home altars of our Mexican poor are true temples of the divine indwelling in the home and should be studied and fostered as an excellent prayer form for today's world.

Because prayer is the language of intimacy, each church is called to propose to its faithful, according to its historical, social, and cultural context, the language of prayer (§ 2663). Yet in spite of all the very legitimate differences among us, and even contradictions (§§ 2791ff), we dare to say together "Our Father." This prayer, uttered together, opens us to God's love for all God's children—no matter how different they might be, whether they are believers or not—and develops within us a love and concern for all people anywhere: those closest to me and those farthest away.

## WHAT HAS TO BE DONE?

The particular challenge for the church in the United States is both fascinating and scary. Our greatest challenge is not the cultural but the inter-cultural and multi-cultural. Even though the Euro-American culture has dominated throughout much of U.S. history and has functioned as the norm for "a good Christian person," today there is no homogeneous culture of the United States, but a mosaic of cultures with a common spirit. We might say that all the cultures of the world are included within the contemporary culture of the United States. Educators, public health officials, advertisers, social workers, politicians, and many others are becoming increasingly aware of this challenge. This is both problematic

and exciting. It is this reality that must come through in any catechetical text of the United States.

It should be noted that we are not alone in this search for
healthy unity amid the diversity within the United States, but we as
church should be at the forefront of these efforts. Precisely because
of our biblical faith, we should be a visionary church that is ahead
of society and not behind it in these present-day struggles. How can
we accomplish this?

*Much has already been done and should be continued.* Catechetical
efforts in the United States have been outstanding, and the various publishing houses with their teams of theologians, catechists,
and liturgists are to be commended for their efforts and risks; they
should be encouraged to continue their exploratory efforts. The
*CCC* can serve as a reference point to see if anything essential is
missing from the totality of our catechetical programs, but it should
not be seen as a negative criticism, or, worse yet, a reason to halt
the marvelous catechetical movement within the United States. But
even the best of materials can be improved and become more
complete by a careful critique in the light of the *CCC* and the
historical-cultural reality of the people for whom the materials are
intended.

Catechetics in the United States can learn a lot from the multicultural efforts of educators, advertisers, and multinational cor-
porations. Our present day catechetical collections can be greatly
improved by including more testimonial stories from our native
Americans, African Americans, Mexican Americans and other
groups. The faith struggles of the minorities of the United States
can certainly enrich our whole U.S. family of faith.

*Recognize with enthusiasm that the United States is a multi-cultural
local church.* Within the multi-cultural fabric of our country and
church, five very distinct groups with particular histories stand
out: (1) the native Americans, with their own rich variety of customs and traditions; (2) the Europeans, who first immigrated and
established the basis of the dominant WASP culture of the U.S.;
(3) the African Americans, who were torn out of Africa and brought
here to serve as slaves; they became Christian in their own ways and,
especially in the independent churches, are an excellent example
of authentic inculturation; (4) the Mestizo/Mulatto Hispanics—
especially the Mexican Americans and Puerto Ricans, who were col-

onized as the United States expanded its borders in the 1840s and
the 1890s, respectively; (5) other immigrant groups, more or less
easily accepted to the degree they resemble the WASP model.

Today there is an urgent need for centers of concerned listening, research, and creative suggestions as to how we can best create a truly inclusive church in the United States. The stories of the
different ethnic groups need to be heard, their cultural expressions
must be appreciated, their prayer forms and religious expressions
must be respected, their special needs must be acknowledged,
and their music, art, and iconography must be encouraged. The
different groups do not want to be judged by some "superior church
group" but want to be acknowledged and appreciated as integral
parts of the total U.S. church. The findings of these centers could
be most valuable for the production of local catechetical and liturgical materials that are faithful to the demands of the *CCC*. The
Mexican American Cultural Center in San Antonio has been doing
this for the Mexican Americans, and after twenty years we feel that
we are just beginning to make a serious start.

In the United States we cannot ignore the strong weight of
the dominant and righteous WASP culture with its racism and
ethno-centrism. Special emphasis must be made throughout the
catechetical texts to attack every notion that consciously or unconsciously promotes white western culture as superior and normative for all others. The Catechism attacks this as the idolatry of
nations (§§ 57; 782; 803; 2112; 2317); this is still one of the great
cultural sins of the dominant culture of the United States and thus
of the U.S. Catholic Church. We must become clearly aware of this
and counter it in every way possible.

*Special attention to issues of social justice.* Precisely because of the
power and wealth of the United States, special emphasis must be
made throughout every U.S. catechism to point out the multiple
faces and causes of poverty and misery both within the United States
and in other countries. The teachings on social justice of our popes
must come through every level of the catechetical process. This is
not an addendum to the doctrinal teachings of our church, but an
integral part of it—carefully tied in to the creedal, sacramental, and
moral life of Christians. Questions of just wages, worker compen-
sation, accessibility of medical care, ecology, ownership, care of
the elderly, treatment of immigrants, sale of arms to poor neigh-

borhoods and countries, waste disposal, exploitation of natural resources, etc. must be included throughout. For the Catechism, charity is necessary but not enough. Christians must work to change the international economic structures that cause so much poverty and misery.

*Pluriform catechesis and liturgy better reflects the richness of God's people.* Whereas a specific catechism might be useful for a particular group at a particular moment, it is my impression that what most of the diverse groups are asking for is not separate and distinct catechisms. This in effect would foster division and segregation. What we want is to be significantly included throughout any of the texts that are developed for the United States—not to appear as an appendix, but as an integral part of the text. This is why every authentic catechetical text must be pluriform; otherwise, it will foster segregation by leaving out the traditionally "unwanted" of our society. For example, the same catechism could describe different baptismal, wedding, and funeral customs associated with the same sacrament, such as the integral role of padrinos in the Hispanic culture. They are all legitimate celebrations of one and the same sacrament. Also, besides the official holy days of the universal church, a section could include some of the special days of other groups, such as Our Lady of Guadalupe and *Dia de los Muertos* (Day of the Dead) for Mexicans and *San Roque* for Italians. A beautiful section could present some of the various Christmas traditions. The students should be encouraged to speak about each other's feasts and celebrate them together. In the celebration of a common feast, we experience ourselves to be a united people.

I suggest the preparation of a simple catechetical/liturgical hymnal that could include several of the most popular and traditional songs of each group. A simple cassette could accompany the booklet and children could gradually learn one another's songs. Religious music is a very important element of the particular religious tradition of each people. It is a way of maintaining communion with the ancestors, which is very important to many groups, and of furthering a joyful fellowship among the diverse cultural traditions. The inter-cultural church should be festive and joyful so that it may be a foretaste and sign of the fullness of God's reign.

People enjoy feasts, and the attendance of Jesus at feasts is evident throughout the gospels. Parishes should celebrate the particular feasts of the people of the parish (e.g. Our Lady of Guadalupe for Mexicans) with all the trimmings of that culture while inviting the entire parish to participate. On the other hand, when the universal feasts are celebrated, such as Christmas or Easter, linguistic and cultural elements of the various cultures represented in the parish should be included.

Furthermore, given the multi-religious reality of the United States and the very positive approach the *CCC* takes to "other religions" (§ 843), it would be exciting to include some of the key feasts of Jews, Muslims, native American religions, and others. These could be presented as giving us other insights into the mystery of God, which could certainly enrich our own since no one expression can exhaust all the possibilities (§ 42). This could be a new and very exciting section—presenting the other great religions not as something false and to be fought against, but as other elements of the ultimate mystery of God. This does not mean that we as Christian Catholics do not have the truth, but it does liberate us from the arrogance of thinking that we alone have it all.

*No one catechetical text will respond to all the needs of the United States. Hence we need to encourage a variety of texts.* This will not be divisive, but enriching.

We are beginning a fascinating moment of planetary communication. I hope and pray that our church may help to bring about a new paradigm of human existence: the reign of the God who watches over all the peoples of the world and who wants us to live in harmony and not in destructive fights and wars. To the degree that we can celebrate our unity in our diversity, we will have something truly new to offer today's multiply divided world. Catechesis and the Catechism, as crucial and important as they are for the life and growth of the faithful, are nevertheless of secondary importance, for they presuppose an effective evangelization through which the whole life and teachings of the crucified and risen Jesus of Nazareth have been accepted by the people, making Jesus the Lord of our life. Catechesis presupposes and builds upon evangelization and conversion. Since the popes, synods, and recent statements of our own U.S. bishops have been calling for a renewed evangelization as the primary and urgent necessity of the entire church at this moment of history, we can surmise that the best of our catechisms and catechesis will be ineffective if Jesus Christ has not been proclaimed and confessed. The church's immediate priority is the most basic presentations, which lead the people to a personal knowledge of Jesus of Nazareth in the fullness of the incarnation of God's eternal word.

# NOTES

## MARTHALER, "THE ECCLESIAL CONTEXT OF THE CATECHISM"

1. Maurice Simon gives a detailed report of the actions taken and not taken by Vatican II regarding catechisms. See *Un Catéchisme Universel pour l'Eglise Catholique du Concile de Trente a nos jours,* Bibliotheca Ephemeridum Theologicarum Lovaniensium CIII (Leuven: University Press, 1992), 132–284. For a briefer account see Berard L. Marthaler, *Catechetics in Context. Notes and Commentary on the General Catechetical Directory* (Huntington, IN: Our Sunday Visitor, Inc., 1973), xvi–xxx.

2. The standard account of the assemblies of the Synod of Bishops is G. Caprile, *Il Synodo dei vescovi.* 8 vols. (Rome: La Civiltà Cattolica, 1968–86). Simon draws on Caprile's work as well as other sources in his report of the action taken by the synod from 1967–85 regarding the Catechism; see Simon, 293–348.

3. Simon, 326; see note 784.

4. For the full text of Pope Paul's closing address and synopses of other synodal documents, see *The Living Light* 15 (Spring 1978).

5. For the full text see Caesare Bonivento, ed., *"Go and Teach" . . . Commentary on the Apostolic Exhortation* Catechesi Tradendae *of Pope John Paul II* (Boston: St. Paul Editions, 1980), 625–91.

6. *Latinamerica Press,* 11 Feb. 1988, p. 6.

7. An English translation of Cardinal Ratzinger's address, "Sources and Transmission of the Faith," appeared in *Communio* 10 (Spring 1983): 17–34.

8. Kasper gave a detailed account of the development of the Catechism in a paper presented to the German Episcopal Conference in March 1984. An English translation, "The Church Profession of Faith: On Drafting a New Catholic Catechism for Adults," appeared in *Communio* 12 (Spring 1985): 49–70.

9. A resume of Kasper's paper appeared in *The [London] Tablet*, Oct. 19, 1985. It was suggested at the time that that paper led to Kasper's appointment as special secretary for the Extraordinary Synod, a position that entailed processing the input from the national and regional episcopal conferences from around the world.

10. Libreria Editrice Vaticana, 1992. The text also appeared in *Il Regno-Documenti* 37 (1992): 450–56. For an English summary of the text see *The Living Light* 29 (Summer 1993): 82–84.

11. The text of *Depositum Fidei* prefaces the Catechism itself.

## KOMONCHAK, "THE AUTHORITY OF THE CATECHISM"

1. See cc. 747–55, especially c. 749, n. 3: "No doctrine of the faith is understood to be infallibly defined unless it is clearly established as such."

2. *Origins* 20 (July 5, 1990): 117–26; for commentaries, see Joseph A. Komonchak, "The Magisterium and Theologians," *Chicago Studies* 29 (1990): 307–29; Avery Dulles, "The Magisterium and Theological Dissent," in *The Craft of Theology: From Symbol to System* (New York: Crossroad, 1992), 105–18; Francis Sullivan, "The Theologian's Ecclesial Vocation and the 1990 CDF Instruction," *Theological Studies* 52 (1991): 51–68.

3. Commenting on the treatment of people who had difficulty in accepting the dogmatic definitions of the First Vatican Council, John Henry Newman criticized churchmen who think "that to believe is as easy as to obey—that is, they talk as if they did not know what an act of faith is." *Letters and Diaries*, XXV (Oxford: Clarendon Press, 1975), 430.

4. *Origins* 22 (January 14, 1993): 526–29.

5. What the pope called the "broadly favorable" response of the world's bishops was detailed by the Commission for the Catechism, which reported that nearly all the bishops thought some such text "necessary, timely, and urgent," 26.8% thought the draft-text was "very good," 51.1% thought it was "good," and 12.1% thought it was "satisfactory with reservations." More than 24,000 amendments were suggested.

6. Bishop Schönborn, while describing the Catechism as "approved by the highest authorities in the church," notes that it "doesn't define any new dogma but expresses the faith in an organic exposition" (Interview, *The Catholic World Report*, December 1992, 58); Cardinal Ratzinger says that it has the authority "proper to the ordinary papal magisterium"; see "Catechismo e inculturazione," *Il regno-Documenti* 37 (November 1, 1992): 588.

7. The comparison of the new Catechism with the *Roman Catechism* was made by Cardinal Ratzinger himself: "Its doctrinal and methodological line enabled it to become a guide in the development of catechesis not only in its own century but for later ones also, respecting and promoting the necessary adaptation to the multiple cultural and ecclesial situations." "Catechismo e inculturazione," 588.

8. *Ibid.*, 589.

9. See *The Catholic World Report* (December 1992): 57.

10. Ratzinger, "Catechismo e inculturazione," 588.

11. See his interview, "I criteri di redazione," *Il regno-Attualità* 37 (November 15, 1992): 585.

12. Perhaps the closest statement to this effect is the explanation in § 20 that "the use of *small letters* for certain passages indicates that

it is a matter of remarks of an historical or apologetical nature or of complementary doctrinal expositions." But a first review of some of these paragraphs suggests that this description does not really address the question discussed above.

13. These observations are confirmed by Bishop Schönborn: "The Catechism has to avoid the impression that all its affirmations have the same level of certainty. But it would not be helpful nor desirable at every step to indicate such levels (*de fide, de fide definita, sententia communis,* etc.). The level of certainty of the doctrines must instead be derived from the context, from the modes of expression, from the doctrinal authority of the affirmation, etc." Schönborn, "I criteri di redazione," 585.

14. Ratzinger, "Catechismo e inculturazione," 588.

15. *Ibid.,* 589.

16. *Ibid.,* 587.

17. *Ibid.,* 586.

18. Earlier the cardinal made a similar point in speaking of those to whom the Catechism is addressed. On the one hand, it has in mind the people of today in their "basic and general aspects"; on the other hand, "it certainly cannot express the differing types of anthropologies that, especially in various systems of meaning, characterize today's world in various geographical places and sociocultural contexts." Ratzinger, "Catechismo e inculturazione," 587.

19. *Ibid.,* 586. I omit here the methodological issues involved in this process of inculturation, on which the cardinal also has important things to say.

20. *Ibid.,* 588.

21. *Ibid.*

## MARTHALER, "DOES THE CATECHISM REFLECT A HIERARCHY OF TRUTHS?"

1. See *L'Osservatore Romano,* Weekly Edition, March 17, 1993, p. 4. Bishop Schönborn cites Thomas J. Reese, ed., *The Universal Catechism Reader: Reflections and Responses* (San Francisco: HarperCollins, 1990).

2. *Origins* 20:22 (November 8, 1990): 358.

3. *Ibid.*

4. Libreria Editrice Vaticana, 1992. The text also appeared in *Il Regno-Documenti* 37 (1992): 450–56.

5. Joseph Ratzinger, "Catechismo e Inculturazione," in *Il Regno-Documenti* 37 (1992): 589.

6. *Ibid.,* 588.

7. See above.

8. Christoph Schönborn, "I criteri di redazione," *Il regno-Attualità* (15 November 1992): 585.

## PHAN, "WHAT IS OLD AND WHAT IS NEW IN THE CATECHISM?"

1. Henceforth abbreviated as *CCC.* I am using the French text and the provisional English translation done by Rev. Douglas K. Clark for the USCC.

2. For an English translation, see *Catechism of the Council of Trent for Parish Priests,* translated into English with notes by John A. McHugh, O.P. and Charles J. Callan, O.P. (New York: Joseph Wagner, Inc. 1937).

3. John Paul II's introductory Apostolic Constitution *Depositum Fidei,* n. 4.

4. As a matter of fact, as pointed out by Berard Marthaler, this four-part structure of the Catechism is only one of the ways in which catechesis is structured. It originated in the sixteenth century and represents a reaction against Luther and Calvin. There were other much older catechetical traditions, such as the catechumenate, the post–baptismal mystagogical homilies, and the threefold structure of Augustine's *Enchiridion*. See "The Catechism Seen as a Whole," in Thomas J. Reese (ed.), *The Universal Catechism Reader: Reflections & Responses* (San Francisco: HarperSanFrancisco, 1990), 22–24.

5. The design of the logo on the cover, taken from a Christian tombstone in the catacombs of Domitilla in Rome, depicts a shepherd (Christ) sitting beside a lamb (the faithful) and holding a flute (the melodious symphony of truth) and a staff (authority). The part on the Creed is preceded by a reproduction of a fragment of a fresco in the catacombs of Priscilla in Rome. It is the oldest image of the Virgin Mary, holding the child Jesus, symbolizing the central mystery of the Christian faith, namely, the incarnation. The part on sacramental worship is introduced by a reproduction of a fresco of the catacombs of St. Peter and St. Marcellinus depicting the encounter between Jesus and the woman suffering from a hemorrhage; the sacraments are like forces coming out of Jesus healing wounded humanity. The part on the decalogue is introduced by a reproduction of the central part of the sarcophagus of Iunius Bassus found under the *Confessio* of the Basilica of St. Peter. It depicts Christ in glory, seated on his heavenly throne, handing out two scrolls (the new law) to Peter and Paul. The last part on prayer is introduced by a miniature of the monastery of Dionysius on Mount Athos depicting Jesus praying to his Father.

6. Avery Dulles, "The Church in the Catechism," in *The Universal Catechism Reader*, 92.

7. For a discussion of communion ecclesiology, see J.-M.R. Tillard, *Church of Churches: The Ecclesiology of Communion*, trans. R.C. De Peaux (Collegeville: The Liturgical Press, 1992).

8. See *Summa Theologiae*, III, q. 65, a. 1.

9. See David Power, "The Sacraments in the Catechism," in *The Universal Catechism Reader,* 110–13.

10. Actually, there are two readings to this creedal formula: Jesus is said to descend "to the dead" (*ad inferos*) and "to hell" (*ad inferna*). For an excellent survey of different interpretations of this obscure phrase, see Berard Marthaler, *The Creed* (Mystic: Twenty-Third Publications, 1993), 170–77.

11. Francis J. Buckley, "Children and the Catechism," in *The Universal Catechism Reader,* 195.

12. For an analysis of five models of contextualization of Christianity and theology, see Stephen Bevans, *Models of Contextual Theology* (Maryknoll, NY: Orbis Books, 1992).

13. See Bernard Lonergan, *Method in Theology* (London: Darton, Longman and Todd, 1972), xi. Two other essays of Lonergan's are particularly relevant to this theme: "Theology in Its New Context," and "Belief: Today's Issues," reprinted in *A Second Collection,* ed. W.F.J. Ryan and B.J. Tyrrell (Darton, Longman and Todd, 1974), 55–67 and 87–99, respectively.

14. Synod of Bishops (30 November 1971), *Justice in the World,* Introduction.

## BORELLI, "THE CATECHISM AND INTERRELIGIOUS DIALOGUE: THE JEWS AND WORLD RELIGIONS"

1. See, for example, the letter of Cardinal Willebrands to the co-chairmen of the Anglican/Roman Catholic International Consultation, *Origins* 15:40 (20 March 1986): 662f.

2. See the explanation by Cardinal Willebrands, "Vatican II's Ecclesiology of Communion," *Origins* 17:2 (28 May 1987): 27ff.

3. For a clear and accurate account of the question, see Francis A. Sullivan, S.J., "The Significance of Vatican II's Decision To Say of

the Church of Christ Not That It 'Is' But That It 'Subsists in' the Roman Catholic Church," *One in Christ* 22 (1986): 115–23.

4. *Directory for the Application of Principles and Norms on Ecumenism,* Vatican City, March 25, 1993: §§ 143–60; published in *Origins* 23:9 (29 July 1993).

5. William H. Lazareth, "Trilateral Reception of Justification by Faith," *Ecumenical Trends* 19:9 (October 1990): 137–44.

6. "Notes on the Correct Way To Present the Jews and Judaism in Preaching and Catechesis," *Origins* 15:7 (4 July 1985): 102ff; see also, *In Our Time,* edited by Fisher and Klenicki (New York/Mahwah: Paulist Press, 1990).

7. *Origins* 21:8 (4 July 1991).

## DOOLEY, "LITURGICAL CATECHESIS ACCORDING TO THE CATECHISM"

1. One of the earliest authors to use the term is Adrien Nocent, "Liturgical Catechesis of the Christian Year," *Worship* 51:6 (November 1977): 496–505; for a discussion of the issues and bibliography see Catherine Dooley, "Liturgical Catechesis: Mystagogy, Marriage or Misnomer?" *Worship* 66:5 (September 1992): 386–97.

2. The provisional draft of the *CCC* had a section on the relationship of catechesis and liturgy but the term "liturgical catechesis" as mystagogy was not in the original text. For critiques of Book Two of the provisional text see Peter Fink, "The Liturgy and Eucharist in the Catechism" (95–108), and David Power, "The Sacraments in the Catechism" (109–25), in *The Universal Catechism Reader: Reflections and Responses,* ed. Thomas J. Reese (San Francisco: Harper 1990). In "Woodstock Catechism Project Revisited," *The Living Light* 29:4 (Summer 1993): 72, Thomas Reese raises the question: "Did the Woodstock project make a difference? Only those who have seen the final draft can answer that question." In my opinion, the current text of Book Two of the Catechism appears to have re-

sponded to many of the criticisms raised by Fink and Power, particularly Power's challenge of "Doctrine or Mystagogy?"

3. Francis Kelly, *The Mystery We Proclaim* (Huntington, IN: Our Sunday Visitor Press, 1993), 72–83, presents a fine reflection on the four pillars.

4. Johannes Hofinger questioned the arrangement of the *Baltimore Catechism* and argued that the sequence itself presents a catechetical message. He stated that the Creed, commandments, sacraments/prayer division of the *Baltimore Catechism* presents the Christian religion "as a well-ordered series of duties or obligations." See "Should the Customary Arrangement of the Catechism Be Changed?" *Catholic School Journal* 55 (January 1955): 4. Another example of the relationship of the ordering of the Catechism to a particular theology is Martin Luther's order of commandments, Creed, prayer and sacraments, which reflected his law-gospel theology. See Gerald Strauss, *Luther's House of Learning: Indoctrination of the Young in the German Reformation* (Baltimore: Johns Hopkins University Press, 1978), 151–76.

5. For a comparison and contrast of the pre- and post-Vatican II understanding of the sacraments, see Peter Fink, "The Church as Sacrament and the Sacramental Life of the Church," *Vatican II: The Unfinished Agenda,* ed. L. Richard (New York: Paulist Press, 1987) 71–81.

6. Albert Houssiau, "La redecouverte de la liturgie par la theologie sacramentaire (1950–1980)," in *La Maison-Dieu* 149 (1982): 27–55, gives an overview of the historical events that isolated liturgy from sacramental theology and indicates how the rites do influence the development of theology.

7. The analogy between the seven sacraments and human growth is traced to St. Thomas Aquinas (*Summa Theologiae* III, 65, 3).

8. A. Kavanagh, "Theological Principles for Sacramental Catechesis," *The Living Light* 23 (June 1987): 317, states that baptism and eu-

charist are fundamental and offers this relationship: baptism (in particular confirmation, penance, and anointing of the ill); eucharist (in particular ordination and marriage).

9. Enrico Mazza, *Mystagogy* (New York: Pueblo Publishing Company, 1989), 1, defines mystagogy as "catechesis on the sacraments, with special reference to the sacraments of Christian initiation and to the deeper spiritual meaning of the liturgical rites."

10. See s.v., "Economy," in Joseph Komonchak, Mary Collins, and Dermot Lane, eds., *The New Dictionary of Theology* (Wilmington, DE: Michael Glazier, 1989), 316.

11. Irene Nowell, "Typology: A Method of Interpretation," *The Bible Today* 28 (1990): 70.

12. See Raymond E. Brown, "Hermeneutics," in *The Jerome Biblical Commentary,* ed. Raymond E. Brown, et al. (Englewood Cliffs, New Jersey: Prentice-Hall, 1968), art. 71, §§ 71–79, for the definition and criteria of the typical sense of scripture and a brief discussion of the relevance of this approach for today.

13. Francis J. Buckley, "What To Do with the New Catechism," *Church* 9 (Summer 1993): 50. Buckley claims that the omission of biblical criticism is not an oversight but that "the authors deliberately chose to ignore criticism of the use of scripture in the preliminary draft." In *Commonweal* 120 (7 May 1993): 17, Luke Timothy Johnson states: "The second thing which impressed me as a biblical scholar is how completely this catechism ignores the results of critical biblical scholarship."

14. Mary Boys, "Scripture in the Catechism," in *The Universal Catechism Reader,* 47. The *New Jerome Biblical Commentary* downplays the importance of typology: "Typology in *NJBC* has been treated more briefly than in *JBC* #71–78 and has been placed under the history of the recent past rather than under the contemporary situation. Although the element of typology is still appreciated, the revival of patristic patterns is not so active now . . ." *NJBC* 71:48, p. 1157. Gail Ramshaw, "The First Testament in Christian Lectionaries," *Worship*

64:6 (November 1990): 496, note 5 states: "Readers may question why I do not use the word typology . . . in my experience the term has lost credibility, being associated for many people with mindless exegesis and anti-Semitic theology."

15. Mazza, *Mystagogy*, 14.

16. John E. Alsup, s.v. "Typology," in David Noel Freedman, editor-in-chief, *Anchor Bible Dictionary* (New York: Doubleday, 1992), vol. 6, pp. 682–85.

17. Andrew D. Ciferni, "Typology/Harmony in the New Lectionary," *The Bible Today* 28 (March 1990): 90–94, and Irene Nowell, "Typology: A Method of Interpretation," *The Bible Today* 28 (March 1990): 70–76.

18. Unfortunately the articles on scripture in the *CCC* contain only two references to liturgy; see §§ 127 and 132.

19. In 1988, the U.S. Bishops' Committee on the Liturgy prepared a statement and set of guidelines, *God's Mercy Endures Forever* (Washington, D.C.: United States Catholic Conference, 1988), concerning the presentation of Jews and Judaism in Catholic preaching and catechesis, in response to the 1985 *Notes on the Correct Way To Present the Jews and Judaism in Preaching and Catechesis of the Roman Catholic Church* (USCC Publication, no. 970).

20. For example, see J.T. Pawlikowski and J.A. Wilde, *When Catholics Speak About Jews: Notes for Homilists and Catechists* (Chicago: Liturgy Training Publications, 1987).

21. A classic work on typology is Leonhard Goppelt, *Typos: The Typological Interpretation of the Old Testament in the New* (Grand Rapids: W.B. Eerdmans, 1982). For more recent comment see Joseph Jensen, "Beyond the Literal Sense: The Interpretation of Scripture in the *Catechism of the Catholic Church*," *The Living Light* 29:4 (Summer 1993): 50–60; Gail Ramshaw, "The First Testament in Christian Lectionaries," *Worship* 64 (November 1990): 496–98.

22. Joseph Jensen, "Prediction and Fulfillment in Bible and Liturgy," *Catholic Biblical Quarterly* 50 (1988): 649.

23. See Ronald J. Zawilla, "The Spiritual Exegesis of Scripture and Contemporary Preaching," Aquinas Institute of Theology Faculty, *In the Company of Preachers* (Collegeville: Liturgical Press, 1993), 76.

24. Geoffrey Wainwright, "Bible et Liturgie: Daniélou's Work Revisited," *Studia Liturgica* 22 (1992): 154–162, remarks: "In my view, typology—precisely in that it respects the concrete history of salvation to which the scriptures bear literary witness—provides an appropriate, and even indispensable, though perhaps not the only, way of relating the Old Testament and the New." See George A. Lindbeck, "The Church's Mission to a Postmodern Culture" *Postmodern Theology: Christian Faith in a Pluralist World,* ed. Frederic B. Burnham (San Francisco: Harper and Row, 1989), 37–55, for a discussion of the need to think scripturally that goes beyond historical-critical exegesis or theological accounts to the patterns and details of the sagas and stories, its images and symbols, its syntax and grammar, which need to be internalized if one is to image and think scripturally.

25. Mark Searle, "Images and Worship," *The Way* 24 (April 1984): 107.

26. Pierre-Marie Gy, "La Liturgie entre la fonction didactique et la mystagogie," *La Maison-Dieu* 177 (1989): 18. In writing on the meaning of the CSL, n. 33, which states that the liturgy also teaches, Gy remarks that "Il est important . . . de ne pas oublier que pour les Peres antiochiens, c'est l'action sacramentelle meme, et non une parole didactique a son sujet, que l'on nomme mystagogie."

27. For a discussion of the nature of liturgical law, see Frederick R. McManus, "Introduction to Book IV, The Office of Sanctifying in the Church," in *The Code of Canon Law: A Text and Commentary,* eds. James Coriden, et al. (New York: Paulist Press, 1985): 593–97.

28. Power, "Sacraments in the Catechism," *The Universal Catechism Reader,* 125.

## FRIDAY, "THE FORMATION OF CONSCIENCE ACCORDING TO THE CATECHISM"

1. Conciliar texts are quoted from Austin Flannery, O.P. (ed.), *Vatican Council II: The Conciliar and Post Conciliar Documents* (Collegeville, MN: The Liturgical Press, 1975). Non-inclusive language appears in the original text.

2. Each paragraph in the *Catechism of the Catholic Church* is numbered. Translations from the French original are taken from the provisional text of the official English translation and are not official at this printing.

3. In the Catechism, "church" often appears to be synonymous with hierarchy rather than with the people of God. This may reflect an ecclesiological inconsistency and/or problem.

4. §§ 1789 and 1970.

5. "(D)irect, willful homicide" (§ 2268); prostitution, where the text says that "those who pay for sex also sin seriously against themselves" and speaks later of "the added sin of scandal" when adolescents and children are involved (§ 2355).

6. St. Thomas Aquinas, *Summa Theologiae,* I–II, 26, 4.

7. In Timothy E. O'Connell, *Principles for a Catholic Morality* (San Francisco: Harper & Row, Publishers, 1990, rev. ed.), the author alleges that the term *synderesis* does not appear in scripture and that "there is no such word in the Greek language" (p. 109). His contention is that St. Jerome misread *syneidesis* and coined a new word to describe the difference he detected between the habit of conscience (*synderesis*) and the act of conscience (*syneidesis*). The Bible does not contain nuance; our subsequent theology does.

8. The three tiers of conscience alluded to in paragraph 1780 are those traditionally found in the moral manuals labeled 1) *synderesis,* 2) moral science, and 3) conscience, sometimes termed *syneidesis,* the Greek word for conscience found in scriptural references. Commonly, contemporary moralists simply refer to Conscience/1, Conscience/2, and Conscience/3. Cf. O'Connell, *Principles for a Catholic Morality,* 109; Richard M. Gula, SS, *Reason Informed by Faith: Foundations of Catholic Morality* (New York: Paulist Press, 1989), 131.

9. O'Connell, *Principles for a Catholic Morality,* 105–09.

10. Later, the Catechism says that "(T)he right to religious freedom is based on the nature of the human person, whose dignity lies in free commitment to the God who transcends the temporal order. Consequently that right persists even among 'those who do not fulfill their duty to seek and adhere to the truth'" (§ 2106).

11. *IV Sent.,* d. 38, a. 4.

12. *Gaudium et spes,* 16.

13. The 1978 National Catechetical Directory, *Sharing the Light of Faith,* recognized the significant place magisterial teachings ought to have in our formation of conscience: "Catholics should always measure their moral judgments by the magisterium, given by Christ and the Holy Spirit to express Christ's teaching on moral questions and matters of belief and so enlighten personal conscience." However, the Directory also acknowledged the limitations of the binding power of magisterial teachings: "It is the task of catechesis to elicit assent to all that the church teaches, for the church is the indispensable guide to the complete richness of what Jesus teaches. When faced with questions which pertain to dissent from non-infallible teachings of the church, it is important for catechists to keep in mind that the presumption is always in favor of the magisterium" (n. 190).

14. Ancient philosophers often used the term *tabula rasa,* blank tablet, to describe the infant upon whom parents, family, society,

and religion would make their marks as values were taught and information communicated.

15. The traditional moral manuals distinguished between a true (correct) and a false (erroneous) conscience. The latter was further divided into scrupulous, perplexed, lax, and pharisaic consciences, depending on the knowledge, will, and, sometimes, the mental state of the person. Cf. Dominic M. Prummer, O.P., *Handbook of Moral Theology* (New York: P.J. Kenedy & Sons, 1957), 58–67.

## NASH, "CATECHESIS FOR JUSTICE AND PEACE IN THE CATECHISM"

1. *Gaudium et Spes,* n. 40.

2. See also John Paul II, *Redemptor Hominis,* nn. 7–8.

3. The Roman Catholic Church, since Paul VI's *Populorum Progressio* (1967), has become increasingly involved in the issue of international justice. John Paul II has written frequently and forcefully on this subject; see also his *Sollicitudo Rei Socialis* (1987), nn. 13ff, and *Centesimus Annus* (1991), nn. 33ff.

4. There is here, however, a brief paragraph devoted to each of the traditional cardinal moral virtues, including justice.

5. Although with the demise of the Soviet Union it might appear that reference to the "international arms race" is out of date, it is still too early to be certain that there will be substantial and permanent reductions in arms expenditures by the major powers. Moreover, the term can also be used to refer to the enormous sums spent by all the world's countries on military weapons.

6. *Catechism of the Council of Trent,* p. 422.

7. There are also sections in the Catechism on the evils of euthanasia and abortion, which were not issues four hundred years ago.

8. In Joseph Gremillion, ed., *The Gospel of Peace and Justice* (Mary-knoll, NY: Orbis Books, 1976), 514.

9. Michael J. Wrenn, *Catechisms and Controversies* (San Francisco: Ignatius Press, 1991), 95.

10. The first question has been dealt with by several documents from the Second Vatican Council. *Lumen Gentium,* in speaking about the relationship between the invisible church of Christ and the visible Catholic Church, declares ". . . many elements of sanctification and of truth are found outside its visible confines" (n. 8).

11. Typical of the "church of sinners but no sinful church" approach is § 829: "While the church has already attained the perfection by which it is without spot or wrinkle in the Blessed Virgin, the faithful still strive to grow in holiness by overcoming sin . . ." Thus the church as a whole expresses the "already" of eschatological fulfillment; its individual members reveal the "not yet" dimension, which awaits completion. I believe that this dualistic division between church and members along the two poles of eschatology is a bit too neat to be satisfactory. See also *Gaudium et Spes,* n. 19.

12. There is, for example, a quotation here from *Lumen Gentium* (n. 48): "The church already on earth is adorned with true but imperfect holiness." There is unfortunately no development of what this corporate imperfection means.

13. See Karl Rahner, "The Sinful Church in the Decrees of Vatican II," in *Theological Investigations VI* (New York: Crossroad, 1982), 270–94. In this article Rahner tries very hard to find evidence in *Lumen Gentium* that the church recognizes that it is sinful as well as holy.

14. See Michael J. Perry, *Love and Power* (New York: Oxford University Press, 1991), 9.

15. Jeffrey Stout, *Ethics After Babel* (Boston: Beacon Press, 1988).

16. *Ibid.,* 165.

17. *Ibid.*, 164.

18. *Ibid.*, 169.

19. In a recent "Style" section of *The Washington Post,* Hillary Clinton pointed to three things many people are missing in their lives today: meaning, connectedness, and power. *The Washington Post,* May 8, 1993, p. D2.

## ELIZONDO, "CULTURAL PLURALISM AND THE CATECHISM"

1. Between the "local church" as a diocese and the universal communion of churches, the documents of Vatican II (*Ad gentes* and *Lumen Gentium*) refer to what I would call a regional communion of churches, that is, those local churches that find a natural unity because of a common language, cultural heritage, and historical journey. However, the case of a local church composed of peoples from various other local churches is something totally new for the church. This is the case in the United States.

2. Jean Marie Tillard, "Theological Pluralism and the Mystery of the Church," in *Concilium* 171 (1984).

3. Term used by Pope John Paul II in Senegal on February 22, 1992, in referring to the European civilizations that took an active role in the slave trade that deported forty million Africans and forced them into slavery.

4. Joseph Komonchak's article quotes extensively from Cardinal Ratzinger's statement bringing out that the one church is only realized in the many local churches.

5. 1977 Synod of Bishops, n. 5.

6. David Tracy, "World Church or World Catechism," 36, in *Concilium* 204 (1984): *World Culture or Inculturation?*

7. Tillard, "Theological Pluralism and the Mystery of the Church," 63.

8. CELAM, Third General Conference (Puebla, 1979), n. 448; Paul VI, *Evangelii Nuntiandi,* n. 48; *CCC,* § 1676.

9. Victor Villaseñor, *Rain of Gold* (Laurel Trade Paperback, 1991).

# CONTRIBUTORS

**John Borelli, PhD,** is a member of the staff of the Secretariat for Ecumenical and Interreligious Affairs, United States Catholic Conference, Washington, DC.

**Sr. Catherine Dooley, OP, PhD,** is associate professor in the Department of Religion and Religious Education, The Catholic University of America. She specializes in liturgy and catechumenate.

**Rev. Virgil Elizondo, STD,** is director of the Mexican American Cultural Center and pastor of San Fernando Cathedral in San Antonio, TX.

**Rev. Robert M. Friday, STD,** is vice-president for Student Life at The Catholic University of America and teaches Christian ethics in the Department of Religion and Religious Education.

**Rev. Joseph P. Komonchak, PhD,** a specialist in ecclesiology, is professor in the Department of Religion and Religious Education, The Catholic University of America.

**Rev. Berard L. Marthaler, OFMConv., STD, PhD,** is Warren-Blanding Professor of Religion, Department of Religion and Religious Education, The Catholic University of America.

**James L. Nash, PhD,** teaches moral theology in the Department of Religion and Religious Education, The Catholic University of America.

**Rev. Peter C. Phan, STD, PhD,** professor of systematic theology, chairs the Department of Theology, The Catholic University of America.

**Rev. John E. Pollard** heads the Office of Catechesis and Leadership Development for Education in the Department of Education, The Catholic University of America.

**Rev. Gerard S. Sloyan, PhD,** professor emeritus of New Testament Studies at Temple University, was visiting professor in the Department of Religion and Religious Education, The Catholic University of America, from 1992 to 1994.